S0-BJH-464

Our Debt to Greece and Rome

EDITORS
GEORGE DEPUE HADZSITS, PH.D.

DAVID MOORE ROBINSON, PH.D., LL.D.

ARCHITECTURE

BY
ALFRED MANSFIELD BROOKS
PROFESSOR OF FINE ARTS

COOPER SQUARE PUBLISHERS, INC.
NEW YORK
1963

NA
260
B7

46674

Published 1963 by Cooper Square Publishers, Inc.
59 Fourth Avenue, New York 3, N. Y.
Library of Congress Catalog Card No. 63-10303

PRINTED IN THE UNITED STATES OF AMERICA

To
F. AND M. A.

Sine amicitia vitam esse nullam

INTRODUCTION

MORE than any of the Arts, Architecture has suffered from misunderstanding and misrepresentation. When it was really vital in the Western World, at almost any period down to the middle of the 18th Century, except in the Dark Ages, Architecture was accepted more or less as a matter of course. There was only one way of doing things, one immemorial tradition and one generally admitted standard of attainment. Accordingly it did not occur to people to be conscious of their architecture. The Greeks, for example, were curiously unconscious of theirs. The poets ignored it, the philosophers despised it as a servile affair, the people generally regarded it as a matter to be taken for granted in the ordinary course of nature. At the Renaissance, it is true, Architecture was studied as an affair of scholarship, and more particularly of technique, but there was no question as between Classic and Romantic because the swing over to Classic was whole-hearted and complete. Unfortunately, in the 18th Century the literary amateur found in this unoffending art an admirable vehicle for discourse and rhetoric, and the " noble patron " of earlier days became the " arbiter elegantiarum " in an Art which he might well have left alone, inasmuch as it had no sort of relevance to his social status. Horace Walpole, in England, treated the Art as an affair of taste and sensibility, the Comte de Caylus " le plus cruel des amateurs," as Diderot called him, treated it as a matter of archæology of which he was to be the official High Priest. Between them they began that process of undermining the foundations of the Art which reduced it more or less to chaos by the end of the 19th Century. It has been considered from the point of view of the Romantic movement, from the point of view of morals, from the point of view of Socialism, from any point of view but that of the ordered disposition of materials for a specified purpose, which is, in fact, the function of Architecture.

In this admirable little volume, Mr. Brooks re-calls attention to the essential basis of

Architecture. The admitted beauty of Greek Architecture was not the result of accident or fashion or caprice, it was attained by steady thought along accepted lines, and what the author very happily describes as " the tireless will of perfection." It took some two or three hundred years to evolve the incomparable Doric of the Parthenon, and rather less to bring to its accomplished beauty the Ionic of the Erectheum. In neither case was there any abrupt incursion of a new motive. Slowly and patiently the Greek craftsman pursued his appointed task, each generation contributing its portion to the sum of ultimate perfection.

In this volume Mr. Brooks has made no attempt to give a detailed account of Greek and Roman architecture. What he is impressing on his students is the spirit at the back of it. From Greek architecture he proceeds to Hellenistic art, with which he deals briefly as the connecting link between the pure Greek architecture of Athens, and the architecture of Imperial Rome. Hellenistic art is an exceedingly interesting, if a very obscure subject; one may regret its lack of purity, and the loss of that austere distinction which stamped the great Doric of the fifth Century B.C. with a quality unique in the history of art; but it is certain that the conquests of Alexander were as epoch-making in architecture as they were in the social and political re-organization of the Nearer East. In the brief period between the death of Alexander and the appearance of Rome on the scene, immense wealth seems to have accumulated in the little principalities of Asia Minor, and their rulers seem to have possessed, not only the leisure and opportunity to use it, but a culture inherited from Greece, sufficiently advanced to ensure that that use was extremely intelligent. Moreover, it was one of the results of Alexander's conquests that the Farther East, after the lapse of unknown periods, was re-introduced to the West. The results were temples of unparalleled magnificence, the first serious undertaking of town-planning on a great scale, a certain sumptuosity of detail which foreshadowed the end of a great tradition, and a remarkable activity of thought, which for the first time set about formulating the principles and canons of architecture. Architecture had become conscious of itself for good or bad, and what Mr. Brooks, in another

connection, calls " free-hand architecture,"
was to be a thing of the past. It is rather
unfortunate that the only survival of this
critical activity is what is summed up in the
famous treatise of Vitruvius. One may be
pretty certain that the keen intellects of
Alexandria went further with the æsthetic of
architecture than the garrulous old architect
who compiled his notes at Rome, in the early
days of the Empire. The *De Architectura*
is a somewhat depressing text book, but it
was treated by the men of the Renaissance
as something approaching a divine revelation,
and much of the stupidity of modern Classic
has been due to the blind following of the
rules of this not very fortunate practitioner.
When the Romans came into Asia Minor,
they seem to have been dazzled by the magnificence of Hellenistic Art. The Corinthian
Capital seemed to them the last word in
architecture, and they imported this more or
less exotic art wholesale into Italy, bringing
back with them Hellenistic artists for the design of their temples and public buildings.
The proceeding was characteristic, and in a
way disastrous, because the Roman failed to
grasp the real quality of pure Greek art, over-

whelmed by the flamboyant charm of its rather degenerate descendant. The glorious temples of Sicily left him unmoved. He might almost have been unaware of their existence. The temple of Diana at Ephesus probably seemed to him a much finer work than the Parthenon. Indeed the Roman seems to have been lacking in artistic sensitiveness. Fine quality in design appealed to him less than sumptuous display and practical convenience. It has been well said by the late Guy Dickins: "The whole fabric of Greek art goes to pieces when it is brought into contact with a purely utilitarian nation like Rome." The "tireless will to perfection" made little appeal to Rome.

But Rome, too, had its contribution to make, and it was a contribution not less vital than that of Greece herself. Moreover — and this is a point that has been seriously misunderstood by writers on architecture, always excepting M. Choisy — that contribution was individual and original. Roman architecture has been represented as a mere vulgar reflection of Greek, and the development or degradation of Greek ornament in Roman hands has been put forward as all that

Rome has to offer. In point of fact it was Rome and Rome alone that opened up the vast possibilities of modern construction. The architecture of the column and the lintel had been carried to a degree of perfection never to be reached again, but it was sterile, — a point is very soon reached at which, apart from steel construction, the column and the lintel either fail of their purpose, or are so wasteful of space and material as to become impracticable. The Roman, practical, masterful, dominated by great ideas, found his way out of this impasse by means of the arch and the vault. He was essentially a constructor. While the Greek architect had been inspired by the majesty of the God whose temple he was building, the Roman was inspired by the service of the State, and so he constructed his magnificent roads, flung his aqueducts over rivers and valleys, and built his basilicas and his theatres, much less concerned with the mysticism of religion than with the present necessities of his fellow-citizens. Moreover, he attacked these problems with an audacity and imagination so splendid that the results rank among the greatest works of architecture ever carried out. Mr. Brooks wisely selects the Colosseum and the Pantheon as typical examples. Only very courageous and very skilful architects could have ventured on such stupendous works as these with no other building materials than concrete, bricks, and mortar. The fact is that Greek and Roman architecture are not in competition, because their aims were entirely different. It was the accident of place and time that led the Roman to adopt, and incidentally to disfigure, the dressings of Greek architecture; he neither mastered its spirit nor attempted to do so; because whether he realized it or not he approached the art of building from a point of view that was almost the opposite pole to that of the Greek. The real greatness of Roman architecture only emerges when the trappings of technical architecture have disappeared, when the columns are broken down and the entablatures destroyed, and we are face to face with the solid basis of reasoned thought in the organic structure that remains. " Roma quanta fuit, ipsa ruina docet." The ideal architecture would be one inspired by the constructive imagination of the Roman chastened by the Greek mastery of abstract form; and this, alone, shews that the literal reproduction of either Greek or Roman buildings will always be a merely futile exercise. It is for this reason that one cannot help regretting the modern tendency to literal copy of the great works of Greek and Roman architecture. Nothing is gained by this, it is not even marking time by dull but honest building. Mr. Brooks quite rightly insists that the lesson of the antique is not its literal reproduction. Its lesson is far more difficult to learn, because it means thinking one's self back to the position of these heroic artists, the attempt to recover the persistent " will to perfection " of the Greek artist, the illimitable courage and far-reaching vision of the Roman builder.

There is a tendency nowadays to ignore the lesson of antiquity, to imagine that it is better for a young man not only to think for himself, but to express himself in terms of his own invention. Thus we get in painting the cubist and that final *reductio ad absurdum* " non-representative art," and in all the arts frantic attempts at originality, which result in mere gibberish. To ignore the art of the past is perhaps even more foolish than to reproduce it literally. If the latter is pedantic, the former is simply childish. In both cases the legacy of the mighty past is misconceived. It is not the letter that is to be sought for, but the spirit that informed it; here only can one find a safe standing in the welter of the modern world.

REGINALD BLOMFIELD

HAMPSTEAD, December 1923.

CONTENTS

[xvii]

CONTENTS

CONTENTS

[xix]

ARCHITECTURE

ARCHITECTURE

I. ARCHITECTURE

That's the noblest art of all the arts

Immortal, though no more; though fallen, great!

THIS line depicts the present condition of Greek and Roman architecture, a matter of fragments. It also pictures the spirit of Greek and Roman architecture, a deathless spirit marching on. To become better acquainted with some of the more important of these fragments and to learn something of the unfailing power of their example, down the ages, most of all on us and our own time, does in a measure describe the purpose of this book. In no sense is it a history of Greek and Roman architecture. While it attempts to trace the influence of the architectural spirit of Greece and Rome upon the building of subsequent days it does not undertake to do so, step by step, inclusively and chronologically. Least of all does it undertake to enumerate the many fine buildings, past or present, intended to be copies, or accurate restorations of Greek and Roman edifices. Important as such buildings are in figuring our debt to Greece and Rome there is an aspect of the subject which is far more important. This aspect concerns the incentive to perfection of beauty and utility which the study of Greek and Roman architecture cannot fail to give; an incentive which has exerted influence, in varying degrees, throughout the centuries and which is mightier today than ever before.

If there be such a thing as the story of a tale that is told being forever retold, in new lands by new people who believe themselves to be rewording the ancient matter when they are inspired by it only and, under the charm of the inspiration, really telling what is as fresh as the dew and as bright as the dawn, — if such a thing may be, then the tale of Greek and Roman architecture, in the days since Greece and Rome fell, is that thing.

Within the surface of Time's fleeting river
   Its wrinkled image lies, as then it lay
Immovably unquiet, and forever
   It trembles, but it cannot pass away!

1. A DEFINITION

The business of architecture is to create, out of given materials, a building of reasonable construction, fit for what it was intended, and beautiful. Reasonable construction means, built in such a way that every part, small or great, shall perform and express its particular function in the economy of the whole, as is the case with natural organisms. Fit for what it is intended is self-explanatory. Beautiful means, so built that the sight of the whole shall be a delight to our eyes. Together these mean what Aristotle meant when he said that all art is based on nature and must, in a sense, keep faith with her. For, before all else, nature is reasonable in her construction and, above all else, dear to the eyes of those who love beauty. Conceived and executed in such a spirit, provided it serve the need of its own day, architecture cannot fail to be fine, and never can grow old.

Architecture, an absolutely unimitative art, in that it has no models as have painting and sculpture, is the art that lends more to the dignity of a civilized people than any other. And this is so because reason and beauty are

[3]

the essence of dignity. On these same grounds, its unimitative character, possible beauty, and reasonableness, it may be called the most creative of the arts, therefore the most human. "None but God and the poet deserve the name creator." Poet, a Greek word be it remembered, meant maker. Few learn the lesson of creating but they who do are the ones who make life better for their fellow men, and their successors. The Greeks and the Romans were preëminent creators, architecturally speaking, though widely divergent in aim and the character of their work. From them, in great part, all subsequent architecture derives, our own in particular. We have fallen heir to the fragments of their buildings. Taken as a whole these fragments constitute a splendid inheritance. The thoughtful restoration of these fragments is the beneficent work of archæology. The effort to penetrate imaginatively the spirit of this inheritance and the wish to use it in the right way, the way of free men filled with respect for tradition but not slaves to it, is the sole road to architectural eminence now, here, elsewhere, ever.

2. GREECE AND ROME

No greater mistake can be made than to assume, as is not uncommon, that architecture began with Greece and Rome, or that it began with Greece and that Roman architecture was merely a coarse and magnified copy of Greek. In architecture, as in all other intellectual and imaginative activities, the Greeks borrowed from their predecessors in civilization, particularly from the Egyptians. So did the Romans in their turn borrow from the Greeks. And so, though unwittingly, the Middle Ages. And so we. It is not the fact of borrowing but the manner of using what is borrowed that constitutes the difference between precious origination and vulgar plagiarism. Neither the Greeks nor the Romans were plagiarists; in architectural parlance, copyists. Neither were they eclectics. Whatever they borrowed they made their own by well-nigh perfect adaptation to their peculiar needs; by improving in a practical way, or making beautiful; usually both. But the Greeks went so far, especially in the creation of beauty, that what they did seemed new and wholly theirs. And it does yet; also unapproachable. On the side of utility the Romans surpassed them. Yet what the Greeks did was not wholly new, though whatever their ideas, and from whatever source, they treated them in such a way that they came forth Greek and nothing but Greek; so beautiful that thenceforth the world called them Greek, utterly forgetting that they were not entirely so to start with. A similar process looking to highly practical ends, and great size, was carried on by the Romans. These processes, in Greece and Rome alike, took a long time. Each dates its history from the same quarter of the eighth century before Christ; 776 B.C. for Greece fixes the first Olympiad: 753 B.C. fixes the founding of Rome. But that Roman architecture which has influenced the whole world did not exist until the time of the Roman Empire, whereas the architecture of Greece reached the perfection of its beauty in the fifth century before Christ, and the perfection of its magnificence during the two centuries following. Asiatic Greece far more than fifth century Greece proper, — Athens, Olympia, Delphi, — gave the impetus to Roman architecture. This being so we shall begin with fifth century

Greek architecture; with Athens as represent-
ing not only the most beautiful individual
buildings produced, but also a very wonderful
ensemble. This unusual and splendid result
by no means follows of necessity upon the
erection of edifices fine in themselves.

The great capital is ever the place in which
to gauge the civilization of a people. There
the best as well as the worst is done; the
gamut is run. So it is that Athens measures
the culture of the Greek world, and Rome the
culture of the Latin. This is why we shall
deal only with them and their best, architecturally speaking, the best of the best, in order
to know what that best was like so that, further, we may recognize its influence upon the
architecture of other peoples and ages, our
own included, and acknowledge intelligently
our part in time's unending debt to them.

3. A WARNING

The tendency to focus our eyes and minds
on contemporary architecture to the neglect
of the past is fraught with twofold danger,
namely, accustoming our eyes to what is not
fine, and starving our minds by neglecting to

furnish them with material on which to build an understanding of what *is* fine. A case, pure and simple, of

> I*f* it would but apprehend some joy
> I*t* comprehends some bringer of that joy.

This is so because the measure of appreciation meted to contemporary architecture, and the tests to which it is subjected, are sure to be unfair wherever there is ignorance of what has been done in the past. This is not to say that we should ignore the work of our contemporaries. We not only cannot do so but we should not try to do so because, obviously, it is not in present work that we should seek the criteria for judgment but in the work of the past; not the dead past, as ignorance calls it, but such a living past as that of Greek and Roman architecture. Art, present or past, is alive only when it has power to influence or move us. It is ignorant not to try to know about the sources of such power; the sort of ignorance which more and more tends to conceit and absurdity the more oblivious we are to the fact. The incentive to architecture is in the present but the inspiration of architecture must come largely from the past; mainly from that fountain-head whence flows the purest and the broadest stream of animating architectural ideas, Greece. That study of the past is essential to present art, alike in producing and in valuing it, is well put by Sir Joshua Reynolds: " Invention is one of the great marks of genius; but if we consult experience, we shall find, that it is by being conversant with the experience of others, that we learn to invent; as by reading the thoughts of others we learn to think." Invention, as used by Sir Joshua, is the same as creation in the sense meant a few paragraphs back. What has been said of Greek and Roman borrowing is also included. Further, the single word, genius, which is more completely descriptive than any other, is here commented on by a man who was himself a genius. Whenever such an one pauses in his practice to talk about art we should give heed as to a most unusual teacher, for the thing is rare.

The following pages deal with the genius of Greece and Rome as it found expression in the most useful and universal of arts, architecture, and with the significance of Greek and Roman architecture to us and our civilization. It is they who developed, as suited to their purposes and civilization perfectly, an architecture which our civilization, after the lapse of two thousand or twenty-five hundred years, turns to more often than to any or all others, for inspiration, and from which it draws, as represented in its individual architectural achievements, constant models. To become better acquainted with the spirit and the body of Greek and Roman architecture is the only way to learn to know our own architecture at its best, and to know how to demand its bettering when not at its best. In proportion as we truly know Greek and Roman architecture shall we recognize our debt to them and learn to rejoice in the works of those of our own builders which most nearly approach theirs, — not as dull reproductions but as living imitations. These only can discharge the debt which never can be paid.

II. HELLENIC BUILDING
A WITNESS OF THE GREEK GENIUS

THOSE only of the works of men live after them in ever-broadening spheres of influence which are bred of a consuming passion, and nurtured in an atmosphere of powerful reason. Greek architecture stands preëminent among such works. It was born of a passion for beauty and it was nurtured by soundness of judgment The first and the last thought of the Greek builders was to use their material to the best possible advantage; — advantage in respect of choice, manipulation and form. Choice as to the kind of material, marble or limestone; manipulation, the way of handling the chosen material, what is known as technique; form, the typical ordinance of parts, columns, entablatures, mouldings. Through custom they established a tradition which has become the embodiment of their spirit. Into it went the best of them, and out of it through subsequent ages has come, and is coming today, the best of them. What that best was, the best the world has ever known, we can get at only through a searching and sympathetic acquaintance with their actual works, not, necessarily, with many of them but, imperatively, with the best of them. Sir Gilbert Murray says in *The Legacy of Greece:* "Doubtless there is in every art an element of mere knowledge or science, and that element is progressive. But there is another element, too, which does not depend on knowledge, and which does not progress, but has a kind of stationary and eternal value, like the beauty of the dawn, or the love of a mother for her child, or the joy of a young animal in being alive, or the courage of a martyr facing torment. We cannot for all our progress get beyond these things; there they stand, like light upon the mountains. The only question is whether we can rise to them. And it is the same with all the greatest births of human imagination." Hellenic building is universally admitted to be one of those births; one of the greatest of them all.

1. THE MEANS OF EXPRESSION: MATERIALS

Within easy reach the Greeks had an unlimited supply of a fine-grained, white marble which lent itself to the most exacting requirements of the stone-cutter, whether builder or sculptor. This material, one of the best in the world, was in general architectural use, and so continued, from the fifth century B.C., on. They also had abundant supplies of first-rate limestone. As a rule when limestone was used, and it was much used, the custom was to cover or surface it with a hard stucco. This was a protection against weathering, and gave the appearance of marble.

The quarries of Mt. Pentelicus supplied the best of white marble, the material of the buildings on the Acropolis of Athens. Good white marble was to be had in many parts of Greece proper, especially at Doliana and on Mt. Hymettus, also on the island of Paros and in Asia Minor; there were beautifully colored and veined marbles as well, but these were little used until Roman times.

Throughout Greece there was ample supply of all the hard and soft woods suitable for building purposes. These the Greeks used in the construction of roofs, though little or nothing is known of the structural methods employed, or of their appearance. Marble tiles served as covering after the middle of the fifth century, but the terra cotta tiling of earlier days was never wholly superseded. Sun-dried brick, though generally employed at first in such buildings as the Heræum at Olympia and the earliest Argive Heræum, is scarcely heard of during the prime of Greek architecture, except for private houses and certain city walls like those of Mantinea. Among building materials metal counted for comparatively little.

With us, as with the Greeks, marble holds first place and limestone is a very important second. The other two materials of monumental significance, granite and brick, were of Roman inclusion and it is from the Romans that we derive the greater part of our ideas about their use alike in respect to the practical and economical, the costly and enduring.

The Greeks well understood how large blocks, in the construction of a building, make for impressiveness, and that they are a device, if rightly used, by which small build-

ings may be endowed with a touch of grandeur.
By extraordinary accuracy in fitting small
pieces together, the drums of a marble column
for example, they built up shafts that looked
like monoliths. Thus they bestowed on them
something of the grandeur which a monolithic
shaft always has; grandeur which our minds
naturally associate with any object which begets thoughts of difficulty overcome; — the
difficulty of finding great pieces, of getting them
out, transporting and setting them up. The
same was true of their limestone shafts, built
of many pieces and surfaced to look like one
piece, a common habit of the present day.

2. TECHNIQUE

The intense care which the Greeks bestowed
upon laying and bonding stone, whether the
blocks of a wall or the drums of a column,
is but one of many proofs of the high regard
they had for technique. It might be too much
to claim that they believed that constant and
intelligent effort to do well the actual work of
building, in a word, good technique, would
lead to designing well, but instances could be
adduced which would go far towards establish-
ing such claim. So exacting were they in the

matter of setting marble and stone that they made almost no use of mortar, preferring to bind the blocks together with inset clamps, usually metal, iron or bronze bedded in molten lead, and not infrequently with wooden dowels. Mortar came into general use after the time of Alexander the Great.

Dry masonry, as masonry laid without mortar is called, requires extreme care in dressing each individual block. This the Greeks did to perfection. For example, when building columns they would leave the vertical surfaces of the drums rough dressed, but the horizontal surfaces, the tops and bottoms of adjacent drums wherever intended to touch, they chiselled and polished to an absolute smoothness and level. Authorities are not wanting who maintain that this process was so fine that it has resulted in the drums, the same is true of the blocks in walls, actually growing together in many cases.

Tenons or projecting knobs were left on the rough vertical surfaces. These served for tackle while lifting the drums into place, and also when grinding drum upon drum in the final fixing. Similar tenons were made use of during the laying up of walls. Buildings so constructed may be said to be erected in the rough. Then, when all was done, the stone-cutters or sculptors, — architecture finished in this manner is a form of sculpture, — would begin at the top and chisel and polish their way downward to the foundations. Such careful methods and wonderful craftsmanship will alone account for the supremely subtle character of the lines and surfaces of the Parthenon. Such care for technical detail is absolutely essential to architecture that shall be perfect on its practical side and, likewise, expressive of a perfect conception of beauty.[1] This is one way of defining the architectural ideal and attainment of the Athenian Greeks in the fifth century before Christ. It is their will to perfection that constitutes the chief item in our debt to them, a debt which men acknowledge in proportion as they understand it, which means, in proportion as they are civilized. Our most precious possessions are the models of perfection which peoples and individuals have left us. And this is so, not because the models can be bodily copied, they should not be so copied, but because of the spirit which they breathe, the spirit of, " go thou and do likewise; " in a word, inspiration.

3. ORDINANCE

Upon one or other of two ways of covering or spanning spaces does all architecture depend. One of these is the beam or lintel. The other is the arch. The Greeks used the beam almost exclusively, though examples of the arch are known among their works. The arch was the Roman way, though the beam played an important part. Of this later. When beams are used, the sole requirement for their support is strength enough to carry their weight. In Greek architecture these supports were of two sorts, walls and posts or, as they are usually called, columns. It was a marked tendency of Greek builders to emphasize the importance of the column, and minimize that of the wall. This they did by veiling, partially screening the walls of their buildings with rows of columns set a little way in front of them. For example, the Greek temple reduced to its simplest terms is a roof of rectangular plan supported on columns, behind, or within which are the walls of the *cella,* the chamber of the temple. Greek architecture was an architecture of columns carrying horizontal beams. It was the two-fold development of this ele-

[18]

mental structure, two-fold in the sense of reasonable and beautiful, that gave rise to what are known as the Orders.

The Order may be defined as the fundamental element or primary unit of the architectural design of Greece. It consisted of the column and its entablature; in other words the supporting part and the parts supported. These gradually took on forms all their own, and these distinctive forms came at last to be universally recognized as right and proper both on the side of construction and the side of beauty. The Orders used in the buildings on the Acropolis of Athens, mid-fifth century before Christ, became canons of good sense and perfect taste and so they remain to the present moment. The study of them is the beginning of education and training in architecture, and no matter how much individual architects or schools of builders, Roman, Renaissance, Modern, from time to time, have varied them, the Greek Orders still dominate our architecture and are still Greek.

The Orders, Doric and Ionic, were named for the two branches of the Greek race, Dorians, settlers of Greece proper, and Ionians who belonged in Asia Minor, Ionia or Asiatic Greece.

The character of the Doric Order, supposed to be an expression of the intellectual temper of the Dorians, was simple, sturdy and severe, whereas that of the Ionic, supposed to be an expression of the intellectual temper of the Ionians, was delicate, intricate and graceful. By the time with which we are dealing, the time that produced those buildings which are, despite their ruined state, potent influences in much of the work of our own day, mid-fifth century before Christ, these two Orders had influenced each other. The sturdy Doric had taken on Ionic grace, though not enough to mar its essential simplicity and severity, while the graceful Ionic had caught something of Doric strength, though not enough to detract from its inherent grace.

About this time the third of the Greek Orders made its appearance, the Corinthian. It was destined to affect Roman architecture more than any other feature of Greek design. From it mediæval columnar forms were, primarily, derived. It became the favorite of the Renaissance. Today, on every hand, in Europe and America, it is the sign manual of architectural importance. Its most characteristic attribute is ornateness. This attribute the

Greeks held in a restraint which only served to enhance the fascination which it exercised. The Græco-Roman and Roman architects, letting go restraint, made the Corinthian Order, what its nature easily admitted of, sumptuous; a unit of architectural design invariably dear to power and wealth when enamoured of elegance and luxury.

Nothing could possibly be simpler in point of construction than the idea of the post and lintel, column and entablature, the Doric, Ionic and Corinthian Orders. So near to absolute perfection, architecturally speaking, as in the final embodiment of this idea, no men, save the Greeks, have ever come. It is the consensus of informed opinion. Among many absorbing facts which present themselves in this connection one in particular challenges interest: the manner in which the Greek architects, having settled on the post and lintel as the unit of architectural design, labored through centuries to perfect its form, first in the Doric and Ionic and finally in the Corinthian. They believed that it was worth every effort of their genius, and never did any single problem in architecture have more or loftier genius bestowed upon it. The result, such hold upon the world as no other unit of architectural design has ever obtained, fully warrants their long, unfalteringly centered thought which would not be deflected for any passing whim of fashion, however alluring. As one contemplates this evidence of the tireless Greek will to perfection, and thinks of the place the Greek Orders hold in American architecture,[2] not to mention European, the White House, the Capitol, the Lincoln Memorial, innumerable public buildings and private dwellings, colonial or of the present hour, small and large, in village and city, Shelley's line assumes a literal and trenchant meaning: " On all this world of men inherits their seal is set." So also does Coleridge's remark to the effect that common sense and the willingness to work are the chief ingredients of genius.

4. THE DORIC ORDER

The Doric Order was the Greeks' favorite. At its best, as seen on the Athenian Acropolis, it united the utmost of strength with extreme delicacy of finish. The Doric column had no individual base, as had the Ionic and Corinthian, but stood, with its brother columns, on a common foundation. This fact tends to deepen the impression of massiveness which is the first impression one gets from a single Doric column, or an entire Doric building. The column which, technically speaking, means shaft and capital, was five and one-half times as high as it was thick through the base. In other words, the diameter of the shaft, a little above its actual base line, was assumed as a unit of measurement for every detail of the order, big or little. It was arranged according to the simplest numerical proportions, the size of every part being proportioned to every other part as well as to the whole, much as is the case with the human body and its parts. The shaft was decorated with twenty shallow, vertical flutes which met in sharp edges. The capital was cut from a single block. Its thickness or height was divided evenly between the lower, circular, flaring part, called *echinus,* and the upper square part or *abacus.* Parallel, horizontal sinkings were cut upon the lower portion of the echinus and a further, single sinking marks the neck of the column just below the heads of the flutes.

The entablature of the Doric Order was

formed of three main parts. The lowest is the series of lintels or beams resting directly upon the columns and spanning the spaces between column and column. It is called *epistyle,* which means that which is on the column, or *architrave,* which means main beam. It had a plain, flat surface. Next, in ascent, comes the frieze. It consists of alternating, supporting blocks or *triglyphs* (so called because of the two grooves with which their faces are channeled and the half-grooves at each edge) and the square *metopes,* which occupy the spaces between the triglyphs and are often sculptured. The topmost layer of the entablature is the cornice. It is composed of two layers of considerably projecting blocks. The relation of height among the three members of the entablature is to the unit of measurement, the diameter of the lower part of the column, as four fifths is to one, for epistyle and frieze each, and three fifths to one for cornice.

The *epistyle* is finished at the top by a narrow projecting band or fillet cut upon it. Below this fillet and under each triglyph there is a flat, bracket-like projection from which depend *guttae,* which means drops. This, as it were, forms a finish for the epistyle and, at the same time, offers the appearance of a base for the frieze. The frieze in turn is similarly, yet with some difference, finished at the top by a series of flat brackets and *guttae* cut upon the under side of the cornice, one above each metope and each triglyph. The cornice terminates in a member of curving outline, the only obviously curved line in the whole order except that of the echinus. It thus appears that the idea of footing and crowning, base and cap, is repeated throughout the parts of the order just as it is emphasized in the whole, and just as it must always be in all good building construction, for it is of the essence of common sense. But the subtlety of line and surface with which all these parts were treated, and the harmony of color with which they were overlaid often lead us to forget that quintessential common sense which lies behind the Doric Order. This no Greek did. To him the perfect union of rational and beautiful, of which nature is the universal symbol, was the final goal of art. He worked out a type which was completely expressive of such union. He believed in his own proverb " all things come by experiment." He was tireless in experimentation until convinced that he had ascertained the model type. That type, in the Doric Order, was sharply defined and admitted of no confusion. It acquired the authority of a sacred tradition but it was not allowed to harden into any mere formalism. Within its limitations individual genius was free to act. And act it did. Witness this typical Doric Order in its similar yet differing forms as used in the Propylæa, gate-house of the Acropolis, and the Parthenon. The differing, hence natural treatments of the order, in these two famous applications of it, illustrate the power of creative architects to make individual application of wise canons hallowed by long testing. It is the proof of Hellenic genius. There are many proofs, but none so absolute. By the Doric Order came that noble simplicity, that serene immobility which are, par excellence, the Greek temple; qualities which enable many men of many minds to see in it the embodiment of perennial youth, and to draw from it everlasting refreshment.

5. THE IONIC ORDER

The Ionic Order is more slender and more decorated than the Doric. Nine and ten times

the diameter of the base give its height to the
column. The entablature is thinner in proportion to the height of the column, and the
column has an individual base of its own which
the wider setting apart of the shafts than with
Doric makes possible, and their greater height
makes necessary. Doric columns were set
near together; Ionic at greater distance from
one another. The shafts were channeled with
twenty-four deeply curved flutes which did not
meet in edges, as with the Doric, but were
separated by narrow strips of plain surface.
The base, particularly what is called the Attic
base, is a sturdy and graceful member which
has, in general, the form of a truncated cone
built up of two thick discs of convex outline separated by a third which is concave.
This base is cut from a single block. Each
part of it, concave and convex, is separated
from its neighbor by a narrow, flat band or
fillet. Carving was applied to the upper member and sometimes to the lower, but not in the
Erechtheum which represents Attic-Ionic at
its best, as the Parthenon does Doric.

The most distinctive feature is the capital
which suggests a sheet of metal rolled up from
both ends, just enough space being left be-

tween the rolls to make fitting possible over the top of the shaft. Thus, at the sides, the rolls are seen in their length, but in front and behind, as ends which are scrolls or volutes. On this rests a thin abacus the sides of which are carved, while the neck of the shaft, between the volutes, and above the flutings, has a collar of carving in low relief. This very charming and rich form of capital, so different according to the point of view from which it is seen, side or front, made the logical returning on the angle of a colonnade impossible, and even a graceful return very difficult. The circular and square forms of the two parts, echinus and abacus, of the Doric capital, the same seen from whatever point, raised no such difficulty.

The epistyle, unlike the corresponding plain member in the Doric Order, was divided horizontally into three parts or faces, each projecting a little beyond the one below. The whole was finished at the top with a narrow band of carved ornament. The frieze, like the epistyle, was a continuous band; sometimes a band of relief carving. The cornice projected much farther, proportionally, than did the corresponding member of the Doric Order. In the examples from Asia Minor where the canons of the Ionic Order were established for Hellenistic, — post-Alexandrian Greek architecture as distinguished from Hellenic, fifth century — the cornice was supported just above the frieze [3] by a dentil course, *i.e.*, a close set row of small square brackets or teeth. In the Athenian use of Ionic during the fifth century this feature was very rarely admitted.

Like the Doric the Ionic was enriched by a liberal use of color and some gilding, the Doric being however without carving. Beside the simplicity, even severity of the Doric, the Ionic warrants the adjective luxuriant, yet it too breaths the spirit of restraint, obedience to an established type, the Greeks' unswerving adherence to the precept, " nothing in excess."

6. THE CORINTHIAN ORDER

The Corinthian Order closely resembles the Ionic in every way except its capital. This feature, taller than in the Ionic, has more or less the shape of an inverted bell. This is covered and decorated with carved foliate forms, acanthus leaves, tendrils and flowers in high relief and full round. The square, thin

abacus is concave in plan on all four sides.
The dentil course under the cornice was never
omitted, while early in the history of the order
the dentils were developed into large brackets
decorated with carving. The circular form of
the capital, and the similarity of its decora-
tions seen from any point of view, did away
with the problem, above referred to, which
always faces the architect who builds a
colonnade that turns an angle. It should be
borne in mind that while the Corinthian Order [4]
is distinctly Greek, — the earliest known example dating from about 420 B.C., — it did
not come into general use until late in the
fourth century. Fanciful, yet sound, are the
lines in which James Thomson characterizes
the three orders. They are eloquent too of
the place these orders had come to occupy in
English architectural thought and procedure
during the first half of the eighteenth century
and, so to speak, when they were beginning to
impose themselves upon America:

> — *First, unadorn'd*
> *And nobly plain, the manly Doric rose;*
> *The Ionic, then, with decent matron grace*
> *Her airy pillar heaved; luxuriant last,*
> *The rich Corinthian spread her wanton wreath.*

[30]

Such an account of the conspicuous characteristics of the three orders as has been given will call to the reader's mind the appearance of each of them; appearance by which he is surrounded on every hand as he walks the streets and squares of any one of the great capitals of legislation or trade in Europe, Britain or the United States. If not perfectly clear as to this appearance all he need do is to look consciously and carefully at what he has long been observing more or less unconsciously, for example, Grant's Tomb in New York; the entrance hall of the Missouri State Capitol; the Post Office in New York. Here, on a magnificent scale, he will see the Doric, Ionic and Corinthian. Elsewhere, on a smaller scale, or on the smallest, in his own porch columns, town or village library, street lamp-posts, he may see thousands of examples. It is the great number not less than the true resemblance to type, despite the numerous wretchedly poor examples, that is impressive and makes us realize our debt to the Greeks of twenty-five centuries ago who gave the world these models of perfection which were to them the symbols, and are to us the mementos, of the well-ordered government of the

Athenian State. To repeat the words of the historian Curtius — he is speaking of Greek architecture and the Greek Orders in general, and of the Parthenon in particular — " it is the Kosmos of the Doric State brought before the senses in stone." And it was one of the first of our American architects, first in quality as well as time, Thomas Jefferson, president of the United States, who did very much to refine and establish the tradition of the orders in this country. He did so because he saw them to be architectural means of intrinsic beauty as well as beautiful symbols of what he would have government and education be in spirit, and in outward expression. The University of Virginia and his house at Monticello bear witness.

7. MOULDINGS

As mouldings are among the smallest things of architecture so they are among the most important. They are those continuous architectural members used for the finish and trim of edges or, to speak figuratively, for softening angles and blending planes. They serve to bind part to part where binding is called for, and they serve to separate parts which should not touch. They are an important means by which architects can lay emphasis upon form. To architecture they stand as the accents of light and shade to painting. They are the source of great beauty and refinement. They are unifying and consolidating elements of design and, being possessed, at the hands of a sensitive composer, of capacity for perpetual adaptation they lend variety and preclude tiresome repetition, the prime virtue and vice of good architecture.

The Greeks attacked the problem of mouldings in the same spirit in which they attacked all other architectural problems. They developed through long, thoughtful experimentation a number of appropriate forms. On these they worked ceaselessly. In time these forms, like the orders, became conventions, never arbitrary conventions, and acquired the force of authority. But under this authority, and within the convention, each individual was free to express his own personality; his own conception of beauty. Further, he was spurred by constant, healthy rivalry to do so to the utmost of his power. The result was an endless variety of shapes, all subjected to a comparatively small number of inexorable patterns; a

46674

variety which conferred upon the Greek building its inimitable charm and vitality. The
quality of reiteration which many people sense
as monotony in second-rate classic buildings,
and in third-rate copies, was utterly lacking
in the architecture with which we are at present
concerned. Orders and mouldings alike were
designed according to laws which governed the
feeling for beauty rather than serving as mathematical expressions of rule, yet numerical relations of a very simple character permeated
the parts and the whole of a Greek temple. In
other words, if every curve of every shaft and
capital and moulding approached a mathematical formula,[5] the result was never more
than an approach, no matter how close an approach. The glory of it all lies in this fact;
the fundamental fact that underlies the works
of nature wherein the union of strength and
beauty confers the last perfection of power.
This characteristic quality of Greek mouldings,
which sets them apart from, and above all
others, as Hellenic Greek architecture is apart
from and above all other architecture, is substantially what the philosopher Heraclitus
means in the sentence: " the hidden harmony
is better than the visible." Keats understood

[34]

and expressed the same thing in the verse:

Heard melodies are sweet, but those unheard
  Are sweeter; therefore, ye soft pipes, play on;
Not to the sensual ear, but, more endear'd,
  Pipe to the spirit ditties of no tone.

The architects of Athens, in the fifth century
B.C., built and carved, *not* to the sensual eye
alone though in all that they did there was a
mighty appeal to that eye. They believed that
the inner sight, essential understanding, is
more affected by architectural attributes which
usually pass unnoticed than by those which are
inescapable. In fine, that the eye sees not
only what it brings with it the power
to see, but more. The works of the Greeks
in marble, architecture and sculpture, one and
inseparable during their prime, are an impressive proof of the fact that only idealists ever
produce ideal art and that nothing is so practical as an ideal. For us, who are seeking
to discover what causes the Greek hold upon
the modern world, the conclusion must be that
as men naturally tend to follow ideals, however
short they fail of attaining them, we tend to
follow the Greek style of building; are following it, however far behind, just as we tend and

mean to follow the precepts of the New Testament, however miserably we may fail. To establish an ideal of behavior in architecture as in any other human concern, and to fix that ideal in the mind of the human race so that it is forever recurring, is to do a very great thing. It is just this that the Greeks did in their architecture; in their orders and mouldings. And they did it for us. Herein is our debt to them.

The most important Doric moulding had an irregular, oval outline. Its profile resembled the line which bounds the long axis of an egg. It is called the *echinus* moulding because its profile and that of the *echinus* of the Doric capital are essentially alike. It had, like all other Greek mouldings of the period, a freehand outline; one that was never mechanically constructed or, for this reason, exactly repeated. In Doric design this moulding, whether used as a continuous band running in a straight line, or around the top of a column thus forming the capital, was decorated with a pattern known as egg and dart, painted in strong colors upon the surface of the marble or prepared stone. The " egg and dart " pattern consists of a series of egg-shaped figures separated from one another by a dart or arrow, the outline of the eggs having the same general form as the profile of the moulding. We here see the application of a principle which the Greeks rarely or never departed from: the idea of making a decorative pattern conform to the shape of that which it decorates. An harmonious and mutually accentive relation between decoration and object decorated is thus established. This relation enhances the beauty and utility of both.

In Ionic architecture the same moulding was used and the same decorative pattern, but with this difference, the pattern was carved. It is almost unnecessary to call attention to the place this moulding and its pattern hold at the present time. Quite aside from its universal use in our architecture, architecture which makes no pretence whatever to being Greek, as well as in that which is avowedly Greek, its application to furniture, picture frames, silver plate and jewelry, to name but a few instances, is also universal. This Greek thing, like many another Greek thing, is part, so to speak, of our stock-in-trade. A striking example indeed of our debt to Greece.

Another, perhaps the most important of all the Greek mouldings, certainly the most generally used moulding today, is one which has a profile composed of a double, continuous curve, convex passing into concave. This moulding when used in situations where actual support is needed, or the idea of support is suggested, has the concave below and the convex above. In positions where actual spreading out in order to make a broader footing, or the appearance of such footing, was required, — what is called a base moulding in distinction to a crowning or supporting moulding, — the convex would be below and the concave above. Endless variants of this double curve were within the reach of an artist draughtsman and an artist carver. Other draughtsmen, notably mechanical draughtsmen and inartistic carvers, the Greeks would not have tolerated.

Various patterns were used for the ornamenting of this double curve moulding. As a rule the ornament was carved. The favorite pattern was what is known as " leaf and tongue," the main bounding outlines of the leaf motif being a free repeat of the profile of the moulding itself. It should not be forgotten

[38]

that the profile of a moulding, when good, always has a structural origin and serves a structural end. This is another way of saying that Greek art, in the present consideration Greek mouldings, exemplified the dominating tendency of Greek thought, the marriage of reason and beauty, the prototype of which procedure they believed they saw everywhere in nature. Like the *echinus* moulding, this of the double curve plays an important rôle today, being present on every hand; for example, in the interior wood finish of houses and public buildings, large or small, and on furniture.

Among other important mouldings which the Greeks either invented outright or treated in such a manner that they became their own and nobody else's, the *roll* should be noted. It has a profile which looks to be half a circle though it is not as a rule mathematically true. It could be made on a large or small scale. Its reverse, a deep concave or bay, is equally important. These two were often combined as, for example, in the composition of the bases of the Ionic and Corinthian Orders already described as the Attic base.

The beak moulding had a section or profile

of hooked shape. The beak proper died away in a compound curve the greatest projection of which lay in a plane well behind that in which the point of the beak lay. This is a perfect form of drip moulding, no water coming from higher up on the building being able to pass the beak and so run down upon the wall or sculptures below, soiling or wearing them. And because it is so deeply under-cut beneath the beak, it casts a line of strongly defined shadow, a thing of great æsthetic value to a thoughtful designer when he wishes to accent some particular part of his construction, as has been said. The Greeks provided for and depended upon such accents just as a draughtsman, or a painter, depends upon heavy lead or color lines when he wishes to bring out salient features or to avoid possible confusion.

A fillet is a moulding of flat section, as a rule, narrow. Its chief use is to separate adjacent mouldings of curved section, or mouldings which are carved. It is important both as an element of division, and of rest by way of contrast. Its effectiveness in such simple and finished architecture as that of the Doric Order is plainly shown by its use at the

top of the epistyle, as a crown, and as a foundation, so to speak, for the triglyphs and
metopes of the frieze. In elaborate architectural design its use as a separator, binder, rest
and contrast is well illustrated by the Greek
sarcophagi in the museum at Constantinople,
particularly that one which is commonly called
the sarcophagus of Alexander. Indeed this
sarcophagus, a Greek building in miniature,
is, in itself, an epitome of the forms of Greek
mouldings and their respective decorative
motifs used profusely but with restraint.
Study of this sarcophagus, like study of the
Parthenon, Propylæa and Erechtheum, the
more pursued, will the more convince us that
to the Greek architect nothing was little or
great, save in respect to dimension; that he
fully appreciated the fact that a perfect whole
must be made up of perfect parts, perfectly
combined. That the Athenians were ready to
pay as much for a strip of egg and dart moulding as for a carved figure is eloquent fact. This
is the secret of that evasive spirit of exceed-
ing beauty which is accepted as the distin-
guishing characteristic of all fine examples of
Greek architecture. It is a spirit which ani-
mates equally minor details, mouldings, and

major details, orders, — call it inspiration, poetic sentiment or any of the many other appellations which wise men, fallen in love with beauty, have invented for it. The orders and the mouldings are at the bottom of the secret of that preëminent richness of architectural effect which the Greeks produced by means at once simple and severe. Together they almost may be said to be Greek architecture, *ipso facto*.

This being so, succeeding peoples and epochs have followed the æsthetic lead of Greece; first the Romans, with slight modification; next the Middle Ages, both in the West and the East, but with great changes due to ignorance and lack of models of what they were following, combined with remarkable native genius which often equalled that of Greece itself; last, the Renaissance which includes the architecture of Europe, Britain, and finally America, from 1400 on, unconsciously, often rudely copying but consciously inspired by Greece, through Rome, whether in failure or success. This is a brief way of saying how the Christian world, through the ages, seeking to house its religious and social activities in reasonable and beautiful edifices, by constantly turning and returning to Greek architecture, has laid itself under an ever-increasing obligation to Greece; an obligation which we shall see as we proceed is due also to Rome in almost equal measure, but for different reasons.

III. ATHENS

THE ACROPOLIS

1. ITS STORY

WITH the final victory of Greece over Persia in 479 B.C., the unbelievable came to pass. It meant that a few Greeks, a mere handful by comparison, had established their independence in the face of a colossal war of conquest made upon their country by Oriental despots. And, further, it meant that the corner-stone of government by the governed was laid, for the Greek commonwealth which thereupon came into being, was an example, to use the words of Lord Bryce, of what men can achieve in the task of governing their own affairs by popular assemblies, the value of which will continue so long as civilized society exists.

Just one year earlier, September, 480 B.C., when the Athenians who had taken the leading part against the invaders returned to their city after the victory at Salamis, they found it desolate; temples and dwellings burned, and defences razed. But if the material conditions of their return were desolation and ruin, the spiritual condition was one of pride, and hope born of assured independence. Great revenues were certain. They were leaders. Intellect and imagination, raised to a high pitch and concerned with everything of interest to a civilized and victorious race of men, were theirs. Finally, virtue of moderation in all things possessed their souls and, for a brief span, dominated their works.

The united effort of the citizens of Athens, from 479 B.C., on, was to make their city first safe; then beautiful. Making Athens, especially the Acropolis, the most beautiful architectural site the world has ever produced, remained for the second generation. Two facts in this connection should never be forgotten. Greek art that had been developing in many places, through a long time, adorned many places in its maturity. But Athens, the Acropolis in particular, not only was itself preeminently adorned, but was the chief ornament of all Greece. There all the various developments of Greek art attained perfection

[45]

in specific works, which works, taken together, made a specific whole that outshone all else, even Olympia and Delphi. The final rush with which the prime of Greek art arrived was like a miracle; less than fifty years. " Nothing that I am aware of in the history of the human intelligence is for a moment comparable to the dazzling swiftness of the ripening of Greek art in the fifth century B.C.," says Lord Leighton.

In 469 B.C., Pericles, greatest of Athenian statesmen, began to govern. " He resolved to make his native city the most illustrious in the world; and he fulfilled his resolution." Under him learning and art prospered to their zenith. The government was democratic. There was hospitality for all. The decade opening with 445 B.C., made the Acropolis what it was, and what it stands for in the history of culture, an ever-active force. Its buildings, upon which Plutarch said there is " a bloom that defies time as if there were in their very stones an immortal spirit and vitality," little better now than a heap of broken marbles, still hold the minds of cultivated men in thrall, and influence the builder's art far

and wide. In no other spot of earth so small
is there so much to fire men's imagination.

2. THE ENSEMBLE

As each building on the Acropolis was meant
to be complete and perfect in itself, all of the
buildings were so placed in relation to one
another as to form a group which, seen as a
whole, should appear complete and perfect in
itself. The central point of interest in this
group, or picture, and the object which, more
than anything else, riveted attention, whether
seen from within the sacred enclosure, from
the city below, from the plains beyond the
city, or from the Ægean main, was the colossal
bronze statue of Athena Promachus, Athena
prepared for war, the work of Phidias. Her
helmet and spear were the high light in the
picture of which she was the center; a center
all the more conspicuous because sculptural,
not architectural; because a human figure,
not a building; a center that could not chal-
lenge by comparison and, therefore, by comparison could neither harm, æsthetically, the
buildings among which she stood nor be
harmed by them. Call it pictorial sense,

power of imaginative composition, consummate knowledge of design; — call it what you will but remember, this creating of a fine ensemble made up of fine parts was a new thing in the world; the thing every great city today is trying to emulate, namely, to make good use of a site as a whole. It was Greek, and Greek of Athens. There, facing straight out over her own gate-house and down the only approach to her sacred places, as Pausanias said, she could see all who drew near, friend or foe. Safe, behind her, to the south the Parthenon; to the north the Erechtheum.

The steep and winding road passed between natural ledges. In the cleft stood the Propylæa set square to the axis of ascent. There was no other way. A wing of considerable size came forward from the north side of the façade, while a corresponding but smaller wing, similarly placed, flanked the south. In front of, and at an angle with this smaller wing, always seen in conjunction with it, stood the beautiful, small temple of Wingless Victory. Together these two made an architectural mass which was a perfect balance for the greater single mass on the opposite side. In this way symmetry and variety were attained at one and the same time, and the Greek doctrine of the one and the many declared. In doing this thing, and other similar things, the Greeks not only set up models of supreme value but laid immovable foundations upon which the most precious, architectural tradition might grow and, in the end, fix itself on the world-mind, as it has.

On passing through the Propylæa into the open spaces beyond, to the right, but at some distance, rose the great and absolutely symmetrical mass of the Parthenon; to the left, but so little to the left as to be almost directly in front, stood Athena Promachus. Beyond, and behind her, its main façade nearly, but not quite, on a line with the façade of the Parthenon, stood the irregular temple called the Erechtheum. Here was another subtle balance produced by dissimilar parts, at once analogous to and wholly different from the balance just discussed in connection with the Propylæa. In this case, the summing up of Athena's statue and the relatively small Erechtheum to equal the greater Parthenon.

3. THE ARCHITECTS

The names of four men shine out from the dimness of time in connection with the Acropolis. The name of Phidias, first of all sculptors, director-general of works, is the brightest. In him the arts of architecture and sculpture were as one. Ictinus planned and built the Parthenon. He was assisted by Callicrates. Mnesicles planned and built the Propylæa. A fifth name should be remembered; that of the painter Polygnotus who, like Phidias, and, centuries later, Michelangelo when building St. Peter's, worked on the Acropolis without pay. Of these men that is true which John Sebastian Bach said of himself: " I compose music for the glory of God and a pleasant occupation."

4. THE PROPYLÆA

The main body of the Propylæa measures about 60 feet as you face it, by 80 in depth, *i.e.,* as you pass through it. The sides were solid walls; the fronts, — one facing upon the Acropolis, the other towards the town, — consisted, each, of six Doric columns, their en-

tablatures and gables. In other words, typical
Doric temple fronts. It was divided, about
two thirds of the way in, by a cross wall.
This wall was pierced by five great doorways,
the widths of which corresponded with the five
intercolumnar spaces of the inner and outer
fronts. The central doorway, like the central
columnar space of each front, was wider than
the side doorways. Through it passed the
road for horsemen and chariots, and through
them the foot paths, leading up to the temple
precinct, or top of the hill. In other words the
main part of the Propylæa consisted of two
Doric porticoes set back to back. The floor
of the outer portico is several steps lower than
that of the inner, due to the slope of the hill
at this point. A rich, coffered marble ceiling,
carried on Ionic columns set in two rows of
three each, covered it. These columns flanked
the roadway and divided the interior into three
aisles. The slender proportions of the Ionic
Order as compared with the heavier proportions
of the Doric, $33\frac{1}{2}$ feet was their height as
against 29 feet for the Doric columns of the
outside, made it possible to give such height
and elegance to this chamber-like portico as
would have been impossible had the Doric

Order been employed. Further, the unusually massive proportions of the Doric Order of the fronts, proportions suitable to a building which, in spirit at least, betook of the nature of protection, prepared the way for a delightful contrast upon entering the lofty, ornate, Ionic interior. Finally, this structure, by keeping separate and combining as it did the Doric and Ionic Orders, filled the mind with the two architectural ideas which were developed individually and on a grand scale in the Parthenon and the Erechtheum; those structures to which the Propylæa was the entrance way. As a prelude, as presaging the two greater things to come, and by announcing the architectural theme of each, the Propylæa was and is without rivals in its kind.

It is in just and entire appreciation of such triumphs as this that we, through our architects, may triumph in the solving of the architectural problems of our day. Not by slavish copying but by free and thoughtful adaptation. Viollet-Le-Duc makes all this very plain: " It is barbarous to neglect the thorough and careful study of Greek art; for Greek art is that which most perfectly subordinated form to the modes of thought and feelings

recognized by the people among whom it
originated, — principles not invented by it, but
which it freely comprehended and unerringly
pursued."

At the right, projecting from the front of the
Propylæa, there was a small wing. Similarly
placed, opposite, but larger, was a pendant
wing. This, because its walls were decorated
by Polygnotus, is known as the Hall of Painting, a sort of National Gallery. Both of these
wings had, each, three Doric columns facing in
upon the roadway. These columns were much
smaller than those of the front itself. This
was a most unusual arrangement, and one
which leads to the belief that Mnesicles was
obliged to abandon a far more extensive plan
which he is known to have had in mind. On
the other hand the reduced size of the wing-
columns is in keeping with the subsidiary character of the parts to which they belong.
Again, by raising these columns on high basement walls, a necessity in order to place them
on a level with the main front to which they
are attached and belong, they were kept duly
impressive. The sense of protection which
these wings give by forming a court, enclosed
and colonnaded on three sides; the effect of

unified yet diversified beauty which the Doric
Order applied differently to the wings than to
the front lends to this fore-court; the contrast
between that order and the Ionic as it loomed
up within and behind the columns of the
solemn Doric façade, all contributed to the
austerely unique charm of the Propylæa which
was absolutely a new thing in the world. It
might not be going too far to name it the father
of modern gateways.

5. THE PARTHENON

The Parthenon [6] is the supreme expression of
the architectural genius of Greece. All first-
rate architects strive to produce, with given
conditions of site, material, and purpose, an
edifice which shall satisfy the purpose, every
part being reasonable and beautiful, the whole
also reasonable and beautiful. The architects
and builders of the Parthenon achieved these
things. It will probably, says Viollet-Le-Duc,
ever be the surest means of initiation into
knowledge of the arts, the most solid ground
of good taste, and consequently of good sense,
for one cannot exist without the other. The
study of Greek antiquity enlarges without con-

fusing the mind. As Lucretius said, the Greek before all other men, " Primum Graius homo," so of architecture it may be said, the Greek temples before all others, the Parthenon first among them.

6. Its Plan

The common base, uppermost of the three equal steps on which stand the columns, measures about 100 feet by 225. Pentelic marble is the material. Humanly speaking the laying out of the Parthenon was perfect. There was but two one-hundredths of an inch difference in more than a hundred feet between the actual measurements of the east and west ends. To get a just appreciation of what such accuracy means think of the opportunities for error and what the sum of slight errors might amount to, often does, in even a hundred foot frontage.

The *peristyle* of the Parthenon, consisting of the encompassing columns, had eight Doric shafts across the ends and seventeen down the sides. Passing between the columns at either end one crossed a floor about ten feet and came to a second or inner row of six Doric columns, raised two steps above the level of the peristyle. These inner columns are more graceful in their proportions than the outer, being 33 feet high with a maximum diameter of $5\frac{1}{2}$ feet, as against $34\frac{1}{2}$ feet high with a maximum diameter of $6\frac{1}{4}$ feet. The end-walls are about twelve feet behind the inner columns, the side-walls being brought forward to form shallow vestibules before the east and west doors. The space between the columns of the peristyle and the side-walls is very narrow.

The entrance was at the east. The main hall measured approximately 115 feet by 75. Thus it had proportions which were substantially the same as those of the building as a whole. The rear hall had the same width, 75 feet with a depth of 50.

The main hall was divided by two rows of columns into side aisles, each about 10 feet wide, and a central aisle about 45 feet wide. The side aisles were returned across the end opposite the door. The ceiling was supported upon Doric columns the arrangement of which was unusual in the Greek world, and new on the mainland of Greece. As single Doric shafts tall enough to reach from floor to ceiling must, of necessity, have had such a diameter as would cover too much floor space, the architect resorted to a double tier, one above the other. The upper column was so designed that the diameter near its base was practically the same as the diameter of the neck of the column below. A series of lintels rested upon the lower columns and made a foundation for those above. Thus the canon of Doric proportions was observed; yet, at first glance, the eye would regard the upper and lower columns as one. Structurally the two did form a single support. In other words two Doric columns, each of correct proportions, but each an individual, were so combined, tapering continuously from floor to ceiling, as to seem a unit.

The west, or rear hall of the Parthenon had its ceiling supported by four Ionic columns. The slender proportions of the order made this possible without too great a sacrifice of floor space. Such light, other than artificial, as the interior of the Parthenon had, came in at the east and west doors. Neither of its halls could have been bright, but for their uses the dim religious light was proper.

7. Its Construction

Let us return to the outside. The columns of the peristyle are $6\frac{1}{4}$ feet in diameter and $34\frac{1}{2}$

feet high. This proportion, despite its sturdiness as compared with the Ionic, is delicate as compared with the Doric of the Propylæa. It is as if the columns of the Parthenon had caught something of the graceful character of the Ionic columns of the Erechtheum close by. The same tendency is to be seen in the entablature. Finally, as if actually taking on Ionic character to the point of direct imitation, there is a carved moulding inserted between the frieze and the cornice.

So far our attention has been given to what may be called the physical aspects of the Parthenon. Let us now consider its spiritual aspects, *i.e.*, some of the causes of its illusive but commanding beauty; a beauty that bears much the same relation to the conventional shapes, placement and proportions of its parts as does the beauty of a lovely face to the universal shapes, placement and proportions of eyes, nose and mouth. The Parthenon is a beautiful and unified whole, the dominant qualities of which are common to all beautiful and unified buildings. To quote from Hamlin's *Enjoyment of Architecture:* " In architectural criticism whether looking to enjoyment only, or through enjoyment to creation, lay or professional, the Parthenon is equally a starting point and a goal. All that men know of good proportion, balance, symmetry, rhythm and that highest quality into which they all finally resolve themselves, harmony, is in it. This is why it figures at the beginning and the end of all architectural teaching. It is like a happy thought consciously or unconsciously recognized as a background to most of our best designing. In a word it has set, indelible, the ideal of harmony in the architectural consciousness of the western world."

At first glance it closely resembles the other Doric building on the Acropolis, the Propylæa, but on more careful examination, the Propylæa is seen to be a much more austere building. This was so for two reasons. The Propylæa had no sculpture. The Parthenon was decorated with sculpture of the most beautiful kind. That the order of the Propylæa is heavier than that of the Parthenon is the other reason. The severely unornamented character of the Propylæa was expressly intended, and suited its position and purpose alike. Temperate magnificence was the key in which the Parthenon was composed. Above the columns of the inner western and eastern ends it had a band of carving in low relief. This was continued down the length of both the side walls at the same level, *i.e.*, at the top of the wall. It is what is known as "*the* frieze" in distinction to the frieze of the order, the frieze which runs around the outside of the building above the peristyle. The subject of "*the* frieze" was the Panathenaic procession, the procession of the best citizenry of Athens bringing their yearly, votive offering of the *peplos*, a fine vestment, to Athena.

8. Its Sculptures

The head of this sculptured procession is over the east door, there where the actual procession after wending its way up the hill, through the Propylæa and along the north side of the Parthenon, entered. Here, in the presence of gods and goddesses, the maidens who wrought the robe make their gift. Behind them, continuing the subject of the eastern frieze, along the north and south walls and across the western end, come priests leading animals of sacrifice, youths bearing sacred utensils and offerings, musicians, old men with olive branches, chariots and charioteers, horses

and knights. Fine as are the scores of indi
vidual figures; fine as is the underlying design
or pattern into which they are worked; un
surpassed as is the technique of it all, the
distinctive feature of this work of matchless
art is its perfect fitness for the place it occupies
in the economy of the architecture as a whole;
— in a word, its suitableness. Sir Sidney
Colvin, warm in praise, cool in restraint,
speaks of it as having " grandly monumental
decorative design and an almost gem-like
finish."

Above the epistyle, on the outside, come
the sculptures of the metopes in high relief.
Here we have a curious repeat of what is at
once similar and dissimilar, in the alternating,
upright flutes of the triglyphs between metope
and metope, and the flutes of the columns as
they cut across " *the* frieze " seen behind and
a little lower down. In other words, as one
stood near the Parthenon and looked up he
everywhere saw rectangles of sculpture terminated to right and left by vertical flutes,
though, as we know, in one case the sculpture
was a continuous band, in the other not, hence
similar and dissimilar. This is characteristic
of Greek design, to make dissimilar things,

which are near together in an architectural composition, such as to appear similar when seen in conjunction and from a distance; individual when seen near to, and by themselves. The Greek designer never forgot the fact that there are two points of view from which a work of architecture is to be looked at; the more or less distant point from which the eye takes in the whole, and the near point which admits only relatively small parts to be seen.

The metope bas-reliefs represent, each, a complete episode; the frieze a continuing pageant. The subjects of the former were drawn from the legendary story of Athens; fights between gods and giants, Greeks and Amazons, the men of Thessaly and centaurs, Trojans, Greeks. The same spirit that ruled the design of the frieze, ruled the design of the metopes in relation to one another, and to the temple as a whole. By this we mean that no human figure, however feminine in its grace, or masculine in its strength; no centaur, however active and noble in its equine qualities, is allowed to withdraw the beholder's thought from the supreme reasonableness of the structural forms and their intrinsic beauty, or from the stimulating sense of tranquil and mighty magnificence which, as it pervades all the parts, is over all the parts, — visible proof of the designer's emotion and the emotion of the people for whom he was, so to speak, the mouthpiece, rather than a literal attempt to portray such emotion. It is thus that architecture, the least imitative of all the arts, of all the arts can best record conceptions of abstract beauty and render fleeting emotion permanent. It is thus that architecture the most concrete and, necessarily, the most logical of all the arts, is of all the arts the most human, because its peculiar province is to give evidence of the power of the mind of man to create order and beauty out of nothing, and to bestow upon them local habitation and a name. For example, to the Parthenon, a work absolutely without prototype in nature but of a quality so closely allied to the organic development of nature, organic is the most truthfully descriptive word that can be applied.

Finally, above the cornice, come the sculptures of the pediments or gables. They are more than life size and in full round. For subject they have the birth of Athena and her victory over Poseidon in the struggle for the supremacy of Athens. Of these figures,

individual or in groups, standing, sitting, re-
clining, in action or in repose, all that has been
said in praise of metopes and frieze, is true.
And more is true. But our present concern
with them is as decorative features, parts of
an architectural whole, and as embodying the
significance of that whole, Athena's temple.
Their simple, massive stateliness enhances the
grandeur of the building of which they are the
crowning glory. Their serenity, whether serenity of calm or of commotion, is monumental,
the last and highest attribute which sculpture
can bestow on monumental architecture; attribute which alone embodies and displays the
sublime.

9. Its Refinements

Nowhere in the Parthenon was there a per-
functory touch. What might, at first sight,
impress one as mere uniformity and symmetry,
upon second sight, and upon all subsequent
examination, impresses one as living variety.
It is this variety of slightly curving line and
surface, slightly slanting line and surface
where one would expect and, ordinarily, find
mathematical straightness and flatness and
verticality, that is meant by the term " refine-

ments " as used in connection with Greek architecture, the Parthenon in particular. These refinements were not suspected until well into the nineteenth century. The earliest to be discovered was the curvature of the lines of the base, epistyle, frieze, cornice and slanting lines of the gables, these curves all being, of course, in vertical planes. To show how slight and how subtle, and to prove the exquisite nature of the workmanship which produced these curves, it is only needful to know that in the length of 100 feet across the base the rise of the curve is less than 3 inches, while in the length of the sides, 225 feet, the rise is only 4 inches.

There are also horizontal curves of the same delicate character. The two fronts of the Parthenon, base and entablature, are concave, *i.e.*, bow in from the spectator. Further, there is scarcely a vertical line or surface in the entire building. The epistyle and frieze slope back while the cornice slopes out. The side walls slope in. The columns are curved in profile, outward from the base through the lower third of their height, then inward, tapering to the neck. They lean inward upon all sides, those, therefore, at the angles necessarily leaning in the direction of the diagonals of the plan of the building. There is a difference of inclination for the side and front columns. The faces of the three great steps of the foundation slope in while the front faces of the abaci of the capitals, like the face of the cornice, incline forward.

The columns of the peristyle are unequal in size, their diameters differing to the extent of nearly 2 inches in an average diameter of something more than 5 feet. In similar fashion the capitals vary 2 inches. The maximum size in shaft and capital occurs at the angles of the temple. There too occur the narrowest spaces between columns, the interval between the angle columns and their nearest neighbors being 2 feet less than elsewhere. The metopes which average 4 feet square vary up to 4 inches. The curved bounding lines of the capitals, are not identical. Many other deviations from mathematical accuracy and rigid symmetry could be cited. And what is, in these respects, true of the Parthenon is true, in varying degree, of much Greek architecture. As if to make this irregularity consummate there are striking exceptions. For example, the Erechtheum has no curvature. And this

is true likewise of the temple of *Nike Apteros,*
which, further, has no tapering to its columns.

That these refinements were intended is an
established fact. It is probable that they were
not indulged in for the sake of correcting
optical illusions, opinion held until very recently, and still expressed by some writers.
What they were for is then a natural question
and one of great importance. Why did men of
such logical minds as the Greeks expend so
much thought and such precious labor upon
these scarcely perceptible refinements, which
never anywhere overstep the strict canons of
Periclean architecture yet make each example
of it unique? The answer is not far to seek.
The Greeks were artists. As such they looked
with care, which means sympathetically and
admiringly, at nature. It was Aristotle we
repeat who said that all art is founded upon
nature and must keep faith with her. He
meant, proceed as she proceeds despite the fact
that such an art as architecture has no models
save in the imaginations of men. The true
meaning of Wordsworth's line, " from nature
doth emotion come," would have been absolutely clear to the masters of the Acropolis
and to " the master of them who know," as

Dante called Aristotle. Now the most striking and universal quality of nature, in all her works, is variety; variety within definite and fixed bounds. The heads and features of men obey a universal law of dimension, proportion and disposition of parts but within the law there is room for endless variation. So with leaves and acorns of oak. So with flowers of violet. So with *Omnia Opera Dei*. To be natural in their art; to avoid monotony while obeying the laws of art, laws of their own making, the outgrowths of common sense and keen sympathy, was to be Greek as the Parthenon is Greek. To express something of the emotion which nature stirred in them, as men, by such works as temples for which nature offered not the remotest suggestion of a pattern, and to express this emotion reasonably, variously and beautifully, was a faith with the Greeks. It taught them to look through nature, the work of the gods, to the gods. Then, to praise the gods by striving to follow after them; never to blaspheme them by vying with them, trying to repeat what they had done as Pygmalion did. This faith bred in the Greeks the habit of looking through their eyes as well as with them. Their art was always a reflection upon nature, never a reflection of nature. Any attempt to build with manual skill only would have meant, to the Greeks, art still-born. Manual skill without love was mockery to them; the death of art. But love and skill in due combination meant the eternal life of art. Their faith is proved by their works: the buildings of the Acropolis before all others, though among many others, ruinous and old in body, yet active beyond all else architectural, in the intellectual life of all times and lands, our own, and here and now. And our not knowing it does not alter the fact.

The difference between a building such as the Parthenon, full of subtle curvatures, imperceptible slope of line and surface, and one in which everything is rigidly mechanical is closely analogous to the difference between an architectural drawing of a fine building and an artist's freehand drawing of that same building. For example, between a good mechanical drawing of a Roman building and Piranesi's etching of the same subject; between a good mechanical drawing of a bit of downtown New York and one of Joseph Pennell's sketches. In one we have fact of knowledge and nothing more. In the other we have interpretation of that fact, on the part of a man whose interpretation, *i.e.*, his interest, is concerned with the human significance, the beauty of fact, not merely fact for its own sake. In the former the letter killeth. The latter is made alive by the spirit. Too little do we realize that architecture is close kin to drawing; that architecture, in no far-fetched sense, means the delimiting of masses and forms against a background. That, further, it means shaping and drawing of details within the mass; the shadows and lights cast and caught by projections, — capitals, mouldings, cornices, just as drawing, in the usual sense, means the counterfeit presentment of these things against a background of paper. The interest and charm of both is, in great degree, due to the variety of the shapes delimited, together with their resulting lights and shadows, the beauty of such variety depending directly upon the care with which each shape is formed and the chances for monotony which it excludes. We can no more expect real impressiveness and beauty of a marble human figure in which one half is the mechanical counterpart of the other, than of a building, or the drawing of a building, conceived in a similarly mechanistic fashion.

[70]

It comes in the end to what is implied by the ancient phrase, an understanding heart; intellectual architecture humanized by love; architecture, or drawing of architecture, done with rule and compass only, or done *con amore*. The Parthenon, or a truly artistic drawing of it; a fine Piranesi or a fine Pennell offer perfect illustrations of what the painter Delacroix meant: "There are some lines which nature will not tolerate; the straight line, the regular serpentine, above all two parallels. When man creates these the elements destroy them. Regular lines are found only in the brain. Then comes the charm of things which are ancient, or in ruins; ruin brings the object closer to nature."

10. THE EVERLASTING LESSON

No straight line in the Parthenon; no parallels; no regular serpentine! Its most precious lesson and its most urgent appeal at present are against sordid mechanism in our own building. The truth is that the Greeks brought their architecture close to nature. It is a sure proof of genius on the part of all architects, if they make their buildings agree with the natural environment, fit the landscape, look as if they had come there, as it were, naturally. Sir Sidney Colvin points this out: " The affinity of Greek nature with Greek art, its power of producing, in the same way, effects of surpassing richness with means of extreme simplicity and severity, is the thing which the Athenian landscape brings continually home to you, in details as well as in general aspect." It is truth that to the Greeks emotion did come from nature, and the fact that their arts, architecture preëminently, are so great is because they found an adequate manner of expressing emotion. Hence their art, like all great art, acts as the reconciler of man to nature and is, as Galsworthy says, man's everlasting refreshment. Herein lies a deep cause for our indebtedness, perhaps the deepest of all. But such indebtedness is more adequately acknowledged, and far more intelligently repaid — was so in the past, is today and will be in the future — by the man whose genius is stirred to emulate the creative procedure of the builder of the Parthenon than by men who seek to copy it, as in the Nashville Parthenon which seeks to imitate not only the architecture but also the sculpture of its

famous prototype.[7] The able but uninspired
builders of such copies are obsessed by the
idea that the needs of the present can be met
by the buildings of the past. The talented
man is often so obsessed. The genius never.
He is inspired by the great past, but he works
for and in the living present. The Lincoln
Memorial is an illustration of this point. The
work of a genius is always new and fresh, and
saves his name to everlasting fame. A good
copyist is saved to temporal respectability.
But the good copy of a fine building is always
better than a poor original; better for him who
makes it, and for the thousands upon whom
it is to exert its long influence.

II. The Erechtheum

That the Erechtheum was built without
curvatures is a fact. William Henry Goodyear
explains this fact by saying: " As regards the
Erechtheum, it may be remembered that it
was built during the Peloponnesian War, when
funds for outlay on Athenian art were not as
plentiful as they had previously been. . . .
There is no doubt that refinements were carried
farther in the Parthenon (aside from the

curvature) than in most Greek buildings, and there is no doubt that the enthusiastic interest of the entire Athenian state, and the unlimited supplies of money resulting from that interest and from the ascendancy of Pericles, are the main explanation."

The Erechtheum is remarkable for the loveliness of its Ionic Order, for the way in which its designers handled a very difficult site, and for its seeming disregard of symmetry, in plan, elevation and detail. Yet it is as impressive in its lack of symmetry, and its departures from custom, as its greater neighbor, the Parthenon, is beautiful in its architectural orthodoxy. The plan is that of an irregular letter T. The upright of the T is the main hall. This hall has six columns across the front. The arms of the T differ materially in their dimensions. They are open porches of identical design so far as structure goes, but diametrically opposed in detail. And not only is the Erechtheum irregular in plan but there is a marked variance among the levels of its three parts, main hall and wings. The difference between the level of the main or east portico, and the porch to the north, amounts to 10 feet. What the Greeks here did in the

exigencies of irregularity they made equal in
fitness and beauty to what they did in the case
of the Parthenon where every condition fa-
vored a formal, symmetrical procedure. The
Erechtheum was never wholly finished.

The order of the east front is very delicate
and elegant but it is surpassed by that of the
north porch. The capital is a marvel with
its complex volutes connected by double lines
which, like the lines of the volutes themselves,
are beyond the reach of all mechanical construction, all mechanical contrivance. Their
convolutions rival the shells of the sea. They
are symbols of what art can accomplish when
it recognizes the necessity for absolute obedience to principle and maintains absolute freedom of action. Like other works of Greek art
in this period they declare the practical wisdom
of Leonardo's aphorism, " ask counsel of him
who governs himself well " — which is the
furthest possible remove from saying " copy
me slavishly."

The capital of the angle column is most
interesting as solving, probably better than
ever before or since, the problem of turning a
corner with the Ionic Order, the defect of which
is, as has been said, the difference between the

volutes of the front and the rolls of the side. When set between the end walls of a portico, the Ionic capital — its length running with the length of the lintel it carries, and its side not easily to be seen, — is well nigh perfect. Failing such conditions the corner or turning capital of the north porch of the Erechtheum is unique in that the outer corner volutes are merged in one greater volute set at an angle of forty-five degrees and somewhat lifted. Thus from either side as well as from the front, the capital appears substantially the same. What one sees is the usual view of a normally set volute and a similar volute placed at more or less of an angle. But even this seems not wholly satisfactory.

The great door leading from the north porch to the interior is the most elaborate designed by the Greeks. The opening is framed in delicately carved mouldings and several flat-faced bands set in receding planes towards the interior. In this latter respect it is like the epistyle of the Ionic Order, a matter of subtle planes over which the light and shadows play, and unlike the massive single-faced epistyle of the Doric. The outer of these surfaces is ornamented with a succession of carved rosettes. The whole is crowned by a carved moulding. This type of door is but one of the many details of the architecture to which it belongs that has been taken over bodily by our day, sometimes well reproduced, sometimes badly. St. Pancras Church in London, the Field Museum of Natural History in Chicago, the Albright Gallery in Buffalo, the Art Museum in Toledo, the Savings Bank of Baltimore are, for example, illustrative of the direct influence for good and the still more precious influence for beauty exerted by the Erechtheum. There is hardly a city of importance in the world which has not some public building with a doorway reminiscent of that in the north porch of the Erechtheum. The same might be said of many fine houses built in the early part of the nineteenth century in our country. This is especially true of the interior work, as in the case of the famous example of Whitehall, near Annapolis.

It is, however, the little south porch of the Erechtheum that delights and amazes all eyes whether of layman or connoisseur. It may be described as breaking the letter and keeping the spirit of every convention and rule. In it human figures take the place of columns.

Hence the name, Maiden Porch. But because they are what they are, and not columns, they stand upon a wall and not on bases like the other supports in the Erechtheum. And because they are human figures, and not columns, the entablature they carry is different from other entablatures which rest on columns. This entablature is compressed from the usual three layers, or parts, into two. Thus, those unfailing features of the Ionic style, bases and three-part entablature, are made to depart from the canon in order to make them harmonize with supports which are not columns. The human figure does not require a columnar base. Neither could it be expected to carry such an entablature as is reasonable upon columns. Yet lest this unusual porch be not felt to be an integral part of the building as a whole, it has been given the same stepped foundation as the rest of the building. At the very start, so to speak, all is tied together; made one. The low enclosing wall on which the figures stand has its own footing and crowning members; is complete in itself. The essence of Greek procedure is maintained in this design which so entirely departs from Greek custom.

The placing of the six figures is similar to the placing of the six columns of the opposite, the north porch, four across the front and two deep at the ends. All look to the front and each stands with one leg straight and one bent. The straight leg is always to the outside so that the drapery over it falls into vertical folds which are suggestive of the flutes of columns. So, to figures distinctly human and lovely, in placement and pose, the architectural nature of their position, and their proper architectural character, as structural members, are preserved. They are a triumph of skill and that which lies behind skill, common sense, expressed in terms of beauty, overpowering love of which is the motive force behind both common sense and skill. There is about them a certain sternness as of perfection which only the greatest art knows.

On the heads of these figures are capitals, but neither Doric nor Ionic. In reality they are headgears which suggest capitals. They are cushion-shaped blocks of echinus form, on which the egg and dart pattern is carved. Above this comes a thin abacus. All that is actually required in the way of capital is here, but in no canonical form. Therefore what is here is appropriate to architecture and not inappropriate to human figures employed architecturally.

The entablature has no frieze, yet the continuous frieze, typical of the Ionic Order, is clearly suggested by the continuous row of disks cut upon the upper surface of the epistyle. In other words the ideas of frieze and epistyle have been merged; the actual members compressed into one. The thin, undercut, projecting cornice, is supported by a dentil course, the dentils of which are more than usually emphasized. Here, if ever, architecture has made concessions to circumstance, and has yielded to requirements imposed from without, but in doing so has produced a result which is consummate art. The animating spirit of this result, shining out from the lovely thing itself, has had no small part in bringing to birth, and ripening our conception of architectural freedom, and in confirming our sense of the difference between such freedom and architectural license. Copies of the Maiden Porch of the Erechtheum, whether in the famous instance of the church of St. Pancras, London, a World's Fair building at Chicago, or elsewhere, however interesting they may be as imitations, are of small relative importance. This porch, the building of which it is a part, and the other buildings on the Acropolis, alike bear witness to the truth of Viollet-Le-Duc's sentence; the Greek observes nature and proceeds as she does; if she has her laws, she also has infinite variety. The major part of our debt to Greece is for giving this truth; this lesson to the world in example and in precept.

12. THE TEMPLE OF WINGLESS VICTORY

It only remains to speak of the miniature temple dedicated to *Nike Apteros,* Wingless Victory, which is set on the high, projecting bastion to the right of the Propylæa.[8] The conspicuousness of its position, together with its small size, richness of design, Ionic Order, and carved frieze, removed it from all possible competition with the great and massive Propylæa by which it stands. The noble and lovely characteristics of each served only the ends of mutual emphasis.

The space enclosed is but little more than twelve feet on a side. It has a portico both at the front and back. These porticoes consist

of *four* Ionic columns of rather more solid proportions and wider spacing than usual. The
entire structure rests on a broad, stepped base
which, because of extreme fineness of the
workmanship, and a certain sense of solidity
not the rule in Ionic buildings, gives the
temple an air of massiveness, disproportionate
to its actual size but exquisitely appropriate to
its position and significance. The continuous
carved frieze, like the stepped epistyle, was
carried along the side walls as well as across
the pillared fronts. This small temple was the
one touch needed on the Acropolis to prove
what the art spirit of Athens, and of Greece,
was in the middle of the " golden," fifth
century. Buildings large and small; regular
in plan and elevation, and irregular; the best
of workmanship and the finest of material; on
every hand innumerable witnesses to respect
for law and love of freedom; finally, the passion for beauty. In the presence of the embodiment of this spirit, either the physical
presence of shattered shaft and entablature, or
the pristine look of the acropolitan group, in
such degree as our imaginations can restore it,
we cannot fail to get a deepened understanding
of the place of Greek art in civilization,

together with that sort of heightened reverence which proves its validity in efforts to better our own work. Here was an art which meets every condition of Rodin's definition: " Art is contemplation. It is the presence of the mind which searches into nature and there divines the spirit by which nature herself is animated. It is the joy of the intellect which sees clearly into the universe and which recreates it with conscious vision."

The reason for studying the architectural art of Athens is well put by S. H. Butcher in his *Aspects of the Greek Genius.* And his dictum is equally applicable to the architectural art of Rome which we are about to consider: " To engage ourselves in a labor of analysis, of logical upbuilding and dissection so much as to reach an appreciation of a thing perfectly done through jealously following the processes of its growth and construction." The consensus of qualified opinion holds that the Greek architecture of Athens in the middle of the fifth century B.C., was " a thing perfectly done." The words of our American artist, Edwin Blashfield, express the value of this art to our time and race and purpose in a manner as unargumentative as it is convincing:

[83]

" If visible beauty is worth while, where may you find it more perfect (or more perfectly pedestalled) than on the Athenian Acropolis? "

Numerous as are the more and less precise copies of Greek buildings, and great as is the dignity which they bestow, — Bank of Ireland, Dublin; Royal Institution, Edinburgh; St. George's Hall, Liverpool; British Museum, London; Court Theater, Berlin; Propylæa, Munich; the great wings of the Capitol, Washington; the U. S. Treasury and the Stock Exchange, New York, — numerous and fine as these are, our debt to Greece is not so much for splendid models to copy as for the example of that transcendent imagination with which the Greek met and conquered every new architectural problem.

IV. HELLENISTIC ARCHITECTURE

THE tendency to divide up the history of architecture into rigidly bounded fields and epochs, convenient as such may be, is dangerous. It is a fact to be kept constantly in mind that architecture like the social and political conditions which it reflects is in constant flux. Architectural customs like all human customs are forever shading off into other customs. Changes which cannot be detected are always taking place. But to discern any considerable change we must look from one age to another, at long range, as it were; from one region to another, in like manner. Those striking differences which then appear are what are commonly known as styles and periods, the convenient divisions just referred to; for example, Greek, or Roman, or fifth century, or fourth century before Christ. Bearing in mind the fact that the transitions from one to the other are slow and delicate, usually imperceptible, and that circumstances do alter cases, we may reasonably avail ourselves of the service of a terminology against which we are warned. The Greek architecture we have considered is called Hellenic; that which followed, and which we are about to consider, Hellenistic. The former bequeathed spirit to the world. The latter gave it examples. The former inspired subsequent ages not so much by a large number of actual buildings as by the immortal tradition which those buildings established; a tradition which was, often, and through long periods of time, unrecognized by those it influenced. The latter furnished Rome with actual models and Rome, in its turn, gave models to the world.

Between 334 B.C. and 323 B.C., Alexander built up his empire. Regions hitherto untouched by Greek influence now felt and owned it while counter influences, especially from the East, had their part in modifying Greek thought and usage. Then, too, architectural problems changed from comparatively small to great. They were problems of building not only large and numerous structures, larger far and far more numerous than those of Athens, but of planning and erecting hitherto undreamt of buildings not to say entire cities, Alexandria and Antioch, for example. Hellenic architecture was, par excellence, the architecture of temples. Hellenistic, Alexandrine civilization, while it continued to raise temples, required civic buildings, both public and private, of every sort, palaces, council houses, theatres, stadia, gymnasia, market places, porticoes, altars, arsenals and commemorative monuments. Architecture which had served comparatively simple ways of life in Athens and other Greek cities during the Hellenic age was called upon to serve a society of unexampled sophistication and complexity during the Hellenistic period. Reasonable and lovely in itself, and powerful to impart reason and loveliness, the architecture of Athens, in no small part because of its perfections, was unable to satisfy the needs of the greater worlds of Macedonian and Roman imperialism. The architecture of Alexander and of the subsequent Hellenistic Greek world, speaking in the broadest terms, the architecture of the third century B.C., as also that called Græco-Roman because produced by the combination of Greek and Roman ideas which followed the Roman conquest of Greece in the second century B.C., was an architecture of expansion. This reached its height under the Roman empire and is what is known as Roman architecture. Its most conspicuous gift was vastness of dimension.

In a few words, the following actual changes took place in architecture looked at from the purely practical point of view. The Corinthian Order became more and more a favorite, and the composite Order, the capital of which was an elaborate blend of the volutes of the Ionic supported by the Corinthian bell-form with its carved foliage, became more and more common. Increase in size went forward hand in hand with lavishness of detail until the adjective sumptuous became the most descriptive word that could be applied to architecture. That freedom of usage which was so perfectly subjected to long, carefully thought out, and accepted canons in Hellenic times often yielded, not without splendid as well as startling results, to what, by comparison, seems license, in Hellenistic and Græco-Roman days. If much that is precious went, a great deal that is necessary and well worth while came. Finally, the arch and the vault made their appearance, though their development, on a colossal scale and in buildings of an all-compelling interest, was destined to await the advent of the engineering architects of imperial Rome. In a word, the architecture of Greece may be said to have originated in and developed from the art of building, whereas that of Rome had its origin in and grew out of engineering.

I. Means of Expression

THE CORINTHIAN ORDER AT EPIDAURUS AND THE CHORAGIC MONUMENT OF LYSICRATES

At Epidaurus, in the fourth century B.C., the Corinthian Order was used for an interior, circular colonnade in a circular building called the *tholos,* the outer, surrounding columns of which were Doric. One of the earliest and finest examples of the Corinthian Order, used externally, is that of the monument of Lysicrates at Athens. This structure, which is practically intact, as the building at Epidaurus is not, is possessed of extraordinary charm. The foliate ornament of its capitals, more elaborate and complex than that of Epidaurus has, in common with it, one marked peculiarity. The way in which the leaves, tendrils, and flowers are treated is suggestive of having been copied from metallic forms, their attenuation, sharpness of edge and suddenness of curve all bringing to mind thoughts of a malleable substances such as metal rather than a brittle substance, marble or stone. This coincides with the tradition that the Corinthian capital was the invention of a bronze worker of Corinth and that he got his idea from seeing the leaves of an acanthus plant grown up about a pot which had been set upon it. Little credence is to be put in this explanation which is as pretty as the thing to which it relates.

The roof of the monument of Lysicrates, cut in one block of marble, is carved to represent tiles of leaf shape. In the center rises a table-like ornament intended to carry a tripod. The intricate loveliness of this crowning feature multiplies as well as carries out to an astonishing degree the rich and exquisite character of the capitals.

2. THE TEMPLE OF OLYMPIAN ZEUS

The most important example of the Corinthian temple on Greek soil, and the earliest that

remains in a fair state of preservation at the
present time, is the temple of Olympian Zeus
at Athens. Begun in the first quarter of the
second century B.C., on the site of earlier
temples which went back to the time of
Pericles, Pisistratus and even Deucalion, it was
not completed until the time of Hadrian in the
second century A.D. Strictly speaking it is imperial Roman.[9] It was gigantic, 135 feet by
354. It had double rows of columns down the
sides and triple across the ends. These
columns were 6⅓ feet in diameter and 56 feet
high, a proportion more solid than was cus-
tomary with the Corinthian Order. The
capitals vary more or less in pattern and execution as might naturally be expected, consider-
ing the history of the temple. They are,
however, typical of the order at its best.
Respect for the structural exigencies of the
case, a slightly flaring block upon which heavy
weight rests, is finely expressed in the way
the foliage is made to fit that block, at one
and the same time emphasizing its shape,
hence function, and also decorating it. It has
little of that vitality of leaf, tendril and flower
which stamp the capital of Epidaurus as a
thing quite by itself. It has no touch of the

fascinating waywardness of the capital of Lysicrates. But it has a solid, decorative character and an evident utility which, in combination, lend it dignity. It is easy to see why it has the strong attraction it has had for modern architects; easy to see why, whether copied outright, or slightly varied, it figures as so important an item in the ever-lengthening sum of our debt to Greece and Rome.

In Asia Minor, Asiatic or Ionic Greece, and in Magna Græcia, Sicily and Southern Italy, during the fourth century before Christ the quality of vast size was, so to speak, grafted upon the parent stem of Athenian, fifth-century, Greek architecture. In the West, Magna Græcia, the Doric Order maintained full sway while the Ionic made little impression. In the East, *i.e.*, along the Ægean shores of Asia Minor, the Ionic Order was dominant, the Corinthian being used occasionally. Interior half-Ionic columns have recently been re-erected in the temple at Bassæ in the Peloponnesus, a temple built by Ictinus, one of the architects of the Parthenon. In this use of attached columns, engaged orders, we see the origin of the pilaster which in our architecture plays so large a decorative part. It was in

Asiatic Greece, too, that a pedestal-like base for temples and other buildings, especially altars, came into use. This base or a flight of many steps took the place of the broad and comparatively low steps upon which fifth-century Greek buildings rested. It consisted of a wall with foundation and crowning mouldings of its own, — the only approach to such a thing in Athenian architecture being the wall, with its own base and cap mouldings, on which stand the figures of the Maiden Porch of the Erechtheum. It is a feature which Roman architects embraced fondly, taking it from the many examples of its use in Etruscan temples, and which, by way of Rome, has come down directly to us from the Romans. The Madeleine in Paris, and many a church and public hall, following its lead, in England and America are witnesses to this.

3. DIANA AT EPHESUS

As the early buildings on the Acropolis of Athens, and elsewhere in Greece proper, were destroyed, so were many of the earlier Ionic temples in Asiatic Greece. Among the latter was the famous temple to Diana at Ephesus,[10] which tradition says was burned on the night of the birth of Alexander the Great, summer of 356 B.C., — that Diana from whose worship St. Paul "persuaded and turned away much people." The work of rebuilding was begun at once. Tradition further says that Alexander offered to pay for the temple provided it bear an inscription to him. The offer was declined. This temple was counted one of the seven wonders of the world. The remains of it are fragmentary, and the restoration is doubtful. None the less, as one of the greatest of buildings in the Ionic Order, and because its remains are exceedingly beautiful, it is an important factor in figuring upon the influence of Greek architecture in modern times. Further, we must not forget that a great architectural tradition, though little is left of the physical facts upon which it was founded, is always a potent force.

Coins showing that the temple of Diana at Ephesus had eight columns with sculptured bases and pedestals across the front, and Pliny's account are the chief authorities on the subject. Not only did the columns stand on sculptured pedestals but the lower part or base of the shaft itself was carved with figures in

relief. There were 127 columns each 60 feet
tall. Of these 36 were sculptured. It is impossible to know just what was the exact
disposition of the latter. But no doubt as to
their imposing beauty can exist in the presence of their remains. The usual dimensions
ascribed to this temple are: 342 feet long and
164 feet wide. It had a double row of columns
on all four sides.

4. APOLLO AT DIDYMA NEAR MILETUS

About 333 B.C. the temple of Apollo [11] near
Miletus was begun, an earlier one having been
burnt by Xerxes and the Persians. It exceeded
the temple of Diana in size and was the largest
temple built in Asia Minor. Strabo says:
" This temple is the largest of all, but, on account of its vastness, remains without a roof,
and there now exist inside and out, precious
groves of laurel bushes." Like Diana at
Ephesus it had double rows of Ionic columns
on all four sides. Like the bases of the
columns of that temple its bases were sculptured, though the decorative scheme of the latter was wholly different. The plan was most
unlike that of Diana at Ephesus, or that of

any other temple of its day, the main hall being open to the sky, and sunken some 16 feet below the level of the peristyle. It was entered by a flight of twenty-two steps which led down to the lower level, from the room behind the portico.

The walls of the unroofed hall were decorated and strengthened by pilasters, each 6 feet broad and 3 feet deep. They stood on a lofty podium and there were in all twenty-one of them. There were engaged Corinthian columns at the entrance. Reference has been made to the carved bases of the outer, surrounding columns. They consisted sometimes of a square plinth upon which rested a twelve-sided base, the twelve sides being panelled and ornamented with bas-relief carvings. On this in turn rested the convex moulding from which the shaft of the order rose. In other cases we have two *trochili* or a *torus* and *trochilus* beneath a circular decorated band.

The influence which the authority of such vast and splendid structures as the temples of Diana at Ephesus and Apollo near Miletus have wrought, despite the wreckage of time and fanaticism of men, the influence of such works upon the architecture of future times,

our own in particular, can hardly be over-
estimated. The fact of these and similar Alexandrine buildings was one of the main sources
of Roman inspiration and the causes of Roman
achievement. From them Rome inherited, and
from Rome we inherit.

5. THE MAUSOLEUM

The tomb [12] of King Mausolus, from whose
name comes our term mausoleum, a word descriptive of any imposing structure for housing
the dead, was built after his death, mid-fourth
century, B.C. For importance, both as a
monument in its own time, and as an influence
upon subsequent architecture, it is to be
classed with the greatest things of the Alexandrine period, and among the most notable
achievements of the Ionic style. The ancients
ranked it among the seven wonders. It was
built by Queen Artemisia in the city of Halicarnassus. Pliny's account together with the
architectural and sculptural fragments which
have survived are the chief sources upon
which to base a restoration. But they are not
sufficient to warrant anything more than a
conjectural restoration. It is certain, how-

ever, that a high base carried a peristyle of thirty-six Ionic columns which bore aloft a twenty-four stepped pyramid or roof crowned with a marble *quadriga,* triumphal chariot drawn by four horses. The fame of the mausoleum was due in no small part to the fact that the best sculptors of the time, such as Scopas, worked on it. Beneath the pyramid roof and within the columns of the peristyle, standing on the floor of the basement story, was a rectangular hall the longer sides of which, according to Pliny, measured 63 feet. The entire platform according to him was upwards of 400 feet around and the quadriga rose to a height of 140 feet. The placing of a peristyle on a basement was done on a gigantic scale for the first time in this tomb. It set a fashion which we follow in the designing of great monuments to the present day, as, for example, in the case of General Grant's tomb. The Scottish Rite Temple in Washington and the Soldiers' Memorial Building in Pittsburgh are two of many buildings which owe their origin to the Mausoleum.

6. Pergamum

As Athens was typical of Greece in the Hellenic period, no one of the short-lived but brilliant kingdoms into which the Empire of Alexander broke up was more typical of Hellenistic Greece than Pergamum.[13] For a hundred and fifty years after the death of Alexander, Pergamum was the most important power in Asia Minor. Its kings kept close touch with all that was Greek and they allied themselves with Rome. On the death of King Attalus the Third, Pergamum went, under his will, to Rome. The part played by Pergamum, a part played by all the Hellenistic cities and kingdoms of Asia Minor, was of great importance in the conquest of Rome by Greek civilization, Greek art. But we must never forget that the Greek art in this instance was no longer the Hellenic art of Athens, in the days of Pericles and Phidias and Ictinus, but rather that Hellenistic Greek art of the age of Alexander the Great. It was Greek art modified in form, and magnified in dimension, by intercourse with the Asiatic civilization of the east coast of the Ægean sea. What that art was, so far as architecture is concerned, was typified by such structures as the temples of Diana at Ephesus, Apollo at Didyma near Miletus, and the Mausoleum at Halicarnassus. Pergamum, probably the chief center of Hellenistic civilization, — Alexandria with its Hellenistic tendencies was always markedly Egyptian, — typified the influences which changed the simple life of Rome under the Republic to the splendid life of Rome under the Empire; typified the influences which changed a Rome of brick into a Rome of marble, to repeat the boast of Augustus.

The acropolis of Pergamum occupied the ridge of an isolated hill, the highest part of which rose more than a thousand feet. This hill curved to the west. A temple of Dionysus, the theatre, and a long colonnade occupied one of the terraces on the side which faced the Ægean Sea. Above the theatre terrace to the right stood the great altar of Zeus and, higher up, the precinct and temple of Athena with the famous library, and still higher the temple of Trajan. Below it on the road up to the Acropolis were the public squares or market places. Lower still was the plain. Other terraces with temples and palaces set among gardens were laid out in interesting fashion on the slope. Here, probably for the first time in history, architects prepared and executed a comprehensive plan which utilized every part and position of a noble site for placing many buildings of varied purpose in complementary relation to one another, and in advantageous relation to the site as a whole. Much care, with highly successful result, was, we know, expended upon the arrangement of the temples on the Athenian Acropolis and their approach, the Propylæa. But apart from its narrow approach, that Acropolis rose as sheer retaining walls or natural cliffs. At Pergamum a steep hillside with terraces up its sharp incline was so built upon as to produce what was at once a homogenous, close-knit and splendid design from base to summit of a long, steeply sloping, concave ascent. Architecture here wholly ceased to be individual in the sense of being an affair of this particular building or that, no matter how fine, and became a matter of one vast group of buildings, a noble city plan in the Roman and the modern sense. Athens when she rose from the Persian ashes was the dawn of the idea of

group and city planning. Delphi and Olympia,
one in a mountain gorge, the other on the
level plain, were complex and not clear arrangements of many different buildings, where
great skill was shown in adjusting what was
new to what was old and sacred and not to be
removed. These and other Hellenic Greek
cities were the slow growths of time. The
planning of each told its story, and the telling
was often highly picturesque but not ordered
from the outset. It was different with Pergamum. Pergamum was the full morning of
civic, ensemble architecture. The whole
scheme was thought out beforehand; every
isolated effect, and the completed effect as a
whole, was foreordained to order and splendor.
Out of such full morning, to continue our
figure, came presently the high noon of city
planning, Rome under the Cæsars.

The great altar of Zeus, really a vast platform for religious ceremonials with a raised
place for the sacrificial fire in the center
measured 500 feet by 300. In the middle of
this platform stood a base-like foundation,
lifted on three steps, 125 feet by 115. On the
west or front, the platform extended forward
at either side into flanking walls. The space

between these walls, 65 feet, was occupied by the twenty-five steps which led up to the level or top where the altar stood. It was enclosed, at a considerable distance and upon three sides, by a wall which had Ionic colonnades within and without. Openings were left in this wall on the side opposite the entrance so that from the rear one could see the altar as well as from in front. The altar itself was a small elevated platform on which burnt the fire of the sacrifice.

The lower part of the basement, really a base complete in itself, with its three steps, mouldings, wall and cornice, was a little under 9 feet high. On this in turn was another set of base-mouldings which formed the foundation for the famous high-relief frieze of giants, as evil, in battle against the gods, as good. This was crowned by a cornice, at the level upon which the altar and its colonnades stood, and up to which the great stairs of the front led. This frieze of colossal figures ran continuously, 420 feet, around the basement, beginning at the stairs on one side and ending at them on the other. It is doubtful if any other work of sculpture on so tremendous a scale was ever attempted. Beside the serene

dignity of the Parthenon frieze, if comparison
is based wholly upon such attributes as
serenity and beauty, the frieze of Pergamum
is a coarse work. But when its scale is considered, and the intent to make a sculptured
decoration that should show to advantage and
tell its story at a distance, and tell that story,
not in terms idealistic such as Phidias employed, but in terms of realism, passion and
primal force, at once human and titanic, the
frieze of Pergamum makes us stand aghast
as before a thing perfect in its own tremendous kind. To know the Parthenon frieze,
and that of Pergamum, and the respective
buildings to which they belonged, to know
these really, which is to know them rightly, is
to know Hellenic and Hellenistic civilization at
their best, and to have very much that is essential for an introduction to an understanding of
the architecture of Imperial Rome. The point
is that Hellenic and Hellenistic, Græco-Roman,
republican Roman, and Roman imperial are
all phases of one unbroken development; a
development which had constantly changing
aspirations amid changing racial stocks in
widely separated regions. A further point is,
the point of this essay, that the architecture

of this unbroken development is the foundation of our own architecture, and it is an architectural history to which we owe a debt so great that it amounts almost to existence itself.

V. ROME

IN 146 B.C., the Romans captured Corinth. This meant that Greece became a Roman province. Whatever occurred architecturally after this on Greek soil was, in reality, only the continuance of what had gone before; the continuance of the architecture of the Alexandrine and Hellenistic epochs, modified by Roman ideas. More and more did the variety of buildings increase, such as public colonnades upon the sides of public squares; council houses; private houses tending to become palaces; the music-hall, the stadium, the theatre. In Magna Græcia, — the great temple of Pæstum, for example, — the Doric Order was always dominant, and the general characteristics of its detail and arrangement of parts followed the type of Doric building in Greece proper but for one notable exception. This exception was increase of dimensions due partly to the necessity of using a coarse-grained stone in place of fine marble.

The same cause led to a heaviness of proportions which, combined with great size, gave the Doric of south Italy and Sicily a massive dignity, a solemnity which is unique. As an influence it is to be counted along with the other influences, Hellenic, Hellenistic, Græco-Roman, both in Greece proper, in Asia Minor, and in Egypt, all of which had their part in the final complex of Roman architecture. It must be remembered that south Italy and Sicily had, by conquest, come under Roman rule as early as 241 B.C., practically a century before the fall of Corinth. That of course meant a close knowledge on the part of Rome of the Doric buildings of this region from an early time. Coming into touch, through conquest, with the Greeks, first in the south and in Sicily, and later in Asia Minor, gave the Romans a chance to see how superior Greek architecture was to their own. The result was that the Romans immediately began to adapt the forms of Greek architecture to their own building.

1. ÆSTHETIC AIMS AND MATERIALS

Down to this period of conquest the people of Italy, and the Romans as the most important people in Italy, had been concerned chiefly with buildings of pure utility; with planning and construction. By nature hard-headed and practical they had neglected the æsthetic and stressed the structural side of architecture. Now to their remarkable works of structural or engineering skill they began to add Greek architectural forms for decoration. As the orders were the chief decorative forms of Greek architecture it was the orders that the Romans added. But as Roman construction dealt with a building principle at complete variance with the principle underlying the Greek conception of the orders, the principle of vertical supports and horizontal beams, post and lintel, the outcome failed of that supreme unity between structural and decorative significance which so signally marked Greek architecture from first to last. The principle of Roman construction was the arch, and the arched roof or vault. For materials they turned gradually away from stone to brick and concrete. This was due partly to the lack of sufficient quantities of stone for their constantly growing needs; partly to rid themselves of the difficulties and expense attendant upon an exclusive use of cut stone. As time ran on they cased their brick and concrete in marble. This should not be taken to mean that the Romans did not use stone and marble in large blocks, as well as quantities, for columns, entablatures and other architectural purposes. They used brick as a casing for concrete, but rarely constructionally.

2. ARCHITECTURAL PURPOSES

Among the Greeks, down to the time of Alexander the Great, temple architecture, including the propylæa leading to temple precincts, was the architecture of chief importance. With the Romans from the days of the Kingdom, increasingly so from the Republic, 509 B.C., sewers, bridges, aqueducts, assembly places, the forum, market places, halls for courts and business were chiefly important. During the later years of the Republic; then, after 31 B.C., and the establishment of the Empire, places for amusement, theatre and circus, bath, palace and commemorative monuments came to the fore. For these latter works the Romans found inspiration in the Hellenistic buildings, other than temples, of Asia Minor and Greece proper. By 250 B.C., the severe and simple architectural requirements of pure utility, along with the earlier ascetic character of republican life in general, were giving way to elegance. This was greatly augmented, as has been said, by the contact with Hellenistic civilization during the period of the Greek conquests. Finally, magnificence and luxury became the chief aim of architecture and we come to the splendors of Vespasian, Titus, Trajan, Hadrian, Diocletian and Constantine, — their great buildings from which the modern world has never ceased to copy and to which its debt is as obvious as it is immense; witness such monumental structures as the Pennsylvania Terminal, New York, (which resembles in design the Baths of Caracalla) the Washington Arch in lower Fifth Avenue, New York City, and others, innumerable.

3. THE ARCH

It is known that the Greeks understood and practised simple arched construction as early as the Romans. The difference between the two peoples, in this important respect, lies in the fact that the Greeks made most sparing use of the arch, while Roman architecture depended on it largely and, increasingly, from the first.

When lintels are laid upon uprights, walls or posts, (the Greek method of spanning and roofing spaces) the sole requirement is that the uprights shall be strong enough to carry the horizontals, together with whatever weights may be placed upon them. In other words, the only force which must be considered is weight in the commonly accepted sense of the word.

When arches are used as the method of spanning and roofing spaces the requirement for their support is twofold; this is due to the fact that the arch exerts lateral pressure, called thrust, as well as weight. To put it in another way, an arch is always tending to push or break itself open on its side or flank. To overcome this the support of the arch must be massive enough to neutralize the thrust. Theoretically an arch is always exerting thrust and therefore in danger, unless it is adequately abutted or buttressed. This fact gave rise to the proverb: "the arch never sleeps." But in practice, it is both possible and easy to do away in part, or entirely, with the thrust of an arch. This depends upon the nature of the materials employed, whether individual pieces, cut stone and brick, or concrete. In the former case thrust may be minimized by the use of clamps between stone and stone, and by strong binding mortar. The tendency in such usage is to tie the parts so firmly to one another that the whole acts more or less like a single piece of material, a monolith or lintel. In the latter case, the use of concrete for arch building, the material is poured wet into a mould. When it has hardened, or "set," it is a single piece and exerts no more thrust than a lintel. But because the element of thrust cannot be wholly dissociated from the arch, the walls and piers carrying arches in Roman work tended to great massiveness which was the part of wisdom.

One other fact here requires mention. When lintels are used, the spaces that can be spanned must of necessity be narrow for the reason that stone and marble cannot generally be had in great lengths and, if they can be, used as lintels, they are apt to crack under very heavy weight. With an arch it is different. Spans many times as long as the longest lintel are possible. Further, provided the abutments are heavy enough, the increase of weight upon the arch only tends to make it more solid. Obviously, however, as the arch becomes broader in span, and supports more weight, its piers and walls must be more substantial. This is why Roman walls and piers are characteristically massive. Both the post and lintel, the Greek structural method, and the arch, the Roman way, have their advantages and disadvantages.

4. THE VAULT

The Romans early developed the vault, *i.e.*, a roof the structural principle of which is the arch and the materials of which are immune from fire and rot because stone, brick, or concrete. Thus it happens that Roman vaulted roofs are numerous today and their nature perfectly understood. For the contrary reasons no Greek roof is left and the whole subject of the Greek roof is a matter of doubt.

The simplest form is the barrel vault. It is

[113]

round arch construction and, like Roman vaulting in general, was geometrical. It was this form of vault which the Greeks knew. The Romans early invented the cross vault, a vault composed of two barrel vaults, semicylindrical surfaces of equal width intersecting each other at right angles. The edges of intersection are called groins and they are necessarily elliptical. Hence this is called the elliptical groin vault. The third form of Roman vault was the dome. It also is a matter of round arch construction, the arches which form it all springing from opposite points in a circular base line. It is usually hemispherical.

One striking characteristic of Roman buildings resulted from the geometrical nature of the forms of Roman vaults. Compartments with parallel sides were necessary for barrel vaults. The elliptical groin vault was used over square compartments. Obviously the dome called for a circular compartment. We shall see as we examine Roman buildings that the architects used these vaults in combination, sometimes two, sometimes all three, and that the outcome was highly desirable because it gave a freedom in complex planning, and admitted of effects both useful and beautiful which otherwise had been impossible. Finally, this freedom begot the invention which, dealing with vaulted construction and concrete, produced the wonderful structures that are at the present time our most generally accepted models both for manner and method.

5. Achievement

Civic architecture, as meaning every variety of building serviceable to great bodies of citizens to whom appearance, safety, utility, and convenience are equally important, was prized and practised by the Romans as it has never been by any other people. This architecture it is that has influenced and is influencing, even largely determining, the aspect of modern British, European and American cities. Unparalleled enterprise and splendor characterized it from the time of Augustus. Perfection of form, proportion and technique, applied to very simple plans upon a limited scale, were the aim of the Greeks. Their works were and are counsels of perfection. The Romans on the other hand broke through these limitations. If, in doing so, they often disregarded what is so precious in Greek archi-

[115]

tecture, they added what is essential to modern civilization, *viz.*, mastery of construction upon a gigantic scale; mastery in piling up incredible masses of building above bafflingly complex plans in such ways as shall adequately serve the needs of great numbers of men, whether a second-century Roman bath or a twentieth-century metropolitan railway station. Imperial Roman architecture had a passion for size, complex plans and sound reason. It was at once the symbol of political power, great wealth and civic use. These were its aims. As such it was dear to the heart of emperor and subject alike. If Greece brought to birth and matured the finest spirit of architecture upon earth, Rome, animated by her architectural spirit, gave that gigantic body of building much of which still defies time and which, as it made mediæval architecture possible, makes modern what we know it. Roman architects did not cease from their labors until, with the completion of the Basilica of Constantine, they had clearly pointed the way which was to lead to the church architecture of the Middle Ages. In the plan of that basilica was the plan of the northern church, and in its cross vaults there was more than a hint of those wondrous vaulting systems which in the Middle Ages France first developed and which all Europe and Britain were quick to take from her.

If, to use Lord Bryce's words, " into Rome all the life of the ancient world was gathered," it may be said with equal truth that out of her has flowed all the life of the modern. Among the many more or less ruinous expressions of the universal spirit of the Eternal City, architectural documentation of her capitalship of the real world, and the world of ideas, vast, massive and decaying piles which to this day communicate her mood of power, a single edifice has come down intact, the Pantheon.

6. THE PANTHEON

How great was Rome, her ruins prove, are the words, translated, which the Italian architect, Serlio, set upon the title page of his treatise, published at Venice in the middle of the sixteenth century. More than two centuries later, Pope, writing of *Urbs Aeterna*, described her as " her own sad sepulchre." Yet there is nothing to suggest death or ruin' about the dome of the Pantheon but only energy, for in its upward, circular sweep it begets thoughts of strength and power only. Rebuilt during the days of Hadrian, in the first half of the second Christian century, its usefulness remains unimpaired; a structure so logically conceived, so carefully thought out; in a word, so well designed that no man has ever undertaken to change it materially, or even wished to. It is the memorial of intelligence; a thing that wears the strange garment of eternity under time as do the Pyramids.

Architecture, like the other arts, can never flourish, much less produce works of permanence and beauty, unless there is genuine and wide-spread interest, first, in building as such, and, second, in the uses to which it is to be put, for without genuineness of emotion no talent, however winning and adaptable, can secure the enduring respect of men. A great architect, like any other great artist, speaks and acts for his fellow men. Sincerity is the corner-stone of all good architecture. The lastingly precious temples, churches and civic buildings of the world are those built by men who professed a faith in which they believed. The architect of this sort of building is a people's spokesman, even though, in name, he serves a despot. His real interests are their interests, but because of superior ability, genius and the devotion of his life, he manages to embody their interests in a way that rightly represents them, and their culture, at their best, and himself at his best. This last necessarily implies the stamp of his personality upon his work. Such stamp is on the Pantheon this minute. And not less is that house of deities, pagan for a time and now for centuries Christian, stamped with the personality of the age which gave it being. Indeed he who sees not the twin-stamp of man and a race of men on the buildings of the past, sees not their meaning and cannot understand them. The Pantheon is the pattern of a people's faith in, and an individual's mastery of a principle of construction to which the intelligence of Rome dedicated itself. It is a work of art which bears the same relation to Roman civilization and the world's culture that the *Aeneid* bears; perpetual reminders, respectively, of the best that was built and the best that was written; really the best that was thought by the Roman people. The two are alike in that their creation belongs to what is often, but ignorantly, called " the dead past "; alike in that their existence implies an active influence upon the present. And this perhaps is the final proof of the value of works of art namely, that with increase of age, their power, measured by their influence upon man, increases. Above all else is this true of Roman architecture. Its place in our present world is analogous to the place Latin has in our daily language. Its influence on St. Sophia in Constantinople, on St. Peter's in Rome where it was Michelangelo's ambition to set " the dome of the Pantheon in mid-air," on the Paris Panthéon, on St. Paul's in London, and on many another building of earlier and modern times is well known.

The Pantheon consists of a hemispherical dome set above a circular hall 142 feet in diameter. The encircling wall, unbroken save by the entrance doorway, is 20 feet thick. The projecting rectangular portico, a Greek temple front, before the entrance, despite its splendid granite columns, is not happy, considered in relation to the circular plan of the building. Neither is the vertical plane of this temple front as seen against the curving wall of the rotunda behind it. Straight and curving lines of the plan, flat and curving surfaces of the elevation do not agree. Their union is a mere juncture. They touch but they do not combine. They are the disjointed parts of a vast mass, not the united parts of a vast whole. Unity is lacking. They present an intensely interesting aspect, and they raise a profoundly interesting question as to the nature and cause of beauty; the necessity of harmony among the parts.

But it is the dome, and the rotunda covered by the dome, the interior, not the exterior, of the Pantheon that is so wonderful, because at once so simple and so vast. It is as one passes in at the forty-foot doorway with its twenty-foot jambs, the original bronze casting still in place, and the original bronze valves, oldest and finest in Rome, that you see how it came about that Hadrian, even among the Romans, got the title " greatest builder of them all."

The wall of the rotunda rises 70 feet above the floor. From this level the dome springs. The crown of the dome is 70 feet higher still. It is a fact worthy of notice that the rotunda would just contain another hemisphere, inverted, like that which is the dome. The entire building is thus, as it were, dominated by a single vast sphere. It is the expression of this dominant conception of simple and mathematically harmonious relationships applied on a colossal scale that makes the interior of the Pantheon unique and impressive.

The wall of the rotunda, and the dome, are divided horizontally into two and five divisions, respectively. These divisions or bands are not of equal height. The lower division of the rotunda, really the first story, is considerably higher than the upper. The two are distinctly separated by a strip of undecorated surface. The lower wall is differentiated from the upper by having seven deep recesses or niches cut back into the thickness of the wall. Three of these are curved on plan and four are rectangular. They add greatly to the sense of lateral spaciousness, floor area. The upper story of this wall is practically flat. It has no niches. The contrast thus produced is most effective. While upper and lower stories are structurally different, their decorative details are identical in spirit. Coupled Corinthian columns stand at the entrance while Corinthian pilasters flank the angle of each niche. The same scheme is repeated above with pilasters. The result is unity of whole and, within it, variety of parts; insurance against monotony, that deadliest of architectural sins; a peculiarly Roman and modern sin. Just because the wall-surface of the Pantheon, 70 feet high and 425 round, is so immense the columns and pilasters with which it is treated lose structural significance, the significance of supporting members, and are thought of as being decorative only. In other words, they are purely ornamental. The good of all this is that the dome does not appear to be carried upon columns, as in reality it could not be, but upon a mighty wall as it is.

The dome, as has been said, is divided into five horizontal bands or rings and these, in turn, are cut across, in vertical planes, by many similar bands so that its surface, up to within 30 feet of the crown, is treated like a checker board, the squares or sunken panels of which, not perfect squares because laid out on a concave, spherical surface, are moulded into the structure of the concrete itself. These panels or coffers offer a fine example of this characteristic Roman method of decorating vaults. Our method is derived from it. Above the coffering, the dome, smooth-surfaced, draws in to the "eye," a circular opening about 30 feet across. Through it the light pours down abundantly and is distributed

to every part evenly. As there is no darkness
anywhere so there is no glare. A serene light
invests the superlative common sense of it all
with the witchery of fascination.

How was this thing built? It is a question
that has been asked many times, and many
times investigated, but one that cannot be
answered, in every respect, so long as that
about which it is asked remains intact. The
wall, concrete, 20 feet thick, except for the
niches, is cased with continuous series, one
above another, of brick, discharging arches,
i.e., arches in the thickness of the wall itself,
set so that the extremities of every pair touch.
Whatever thrust, if any, one of these arches
may exert is neutralized by the counter thrust
of its next neighbor. To make clear the
arrangement of these arches one need only
think of a perfect ring marked on the ground,
and a series of arched, croquet wickets, wicket
touching wicket, stuck into this ring until the
circle is completed. The spaces beneath these
arches, as well as between them, are filled in
solid, with brick bedded into the concrete.
The structure of the dome is essentially the
same, a complex brick framework covered and
buried in brick concrete. It is composed of a

net which may be thought of as a hemispherical lattice work of arches rising above one another and abutting against the ring of the " eye." Over this lattice, and on it, as a permanent mould, really a skeleton, the builders put concrete, which is different from the usual Roman concrete of pozzolana and crushed stone in that broken brick is also used. The lower part of the dome is much thicker than the upper and, further, the lower part is banked up or weighted with terraces of stone. This diminishing thickness, 20 feet at its springing line and 8 feet at the " eye," together with the weighting, are precautionary measures which sound reason, the crowning Roman virtue, dictated.

The dome of the Pantheon, concave, and shaped like the sky, covers a circular bounding line like that of the horizon. Even the circular floor slightly mounded has something of the convex form of the earth itself which is a sphere. Everywhere the circle and the sphere, whole or in part, dominate the beholder's thought as they dominated the designer's. This is equally the essence of every constructive exigency and every visual appearance. It is as if the very angels of architecture had undertaken to extol circle and sphere in one great, rhythmic symphony of the round. Like all the labors of consummate architects, and every work of nature, it produces a sense of exhilarating calm, and is a profound and consoling proof of the possible truth of the words:

What a piece of work is man! how noble in reason! how infinite in faculty!

The Pantheon proclaims the nobility of Roman reason, and the magnitude of Roman faculty. But, be it remembered, it still declares, just as the architecture of the opening decade of the twentieth century will declare so long as it shall stand, that the world of matter subjected to the control of science is not enough for man; that man cannot live by bread alone. Greater error is not. Proof more absolute of having fallen into it he cannot make than in his architecture; proof made by the Romans again and again, notwithstanding the dazzling material greatness of their accomplishment, attested, for example in the Pantheon. Theirs, like our intellectuality, was cold; a matter of applied mathematics, a dominant desire to serve so-called practical ends, in one word, bigness; this, in everlasting distinction to the sort of intellectuality exhibited by the Greeks before them, and the mediæval French after them. The Greek and French intellectuality always aimed beyond the practical, even as it attained the practical, in the sure faith that an ideal end is the only possible practical end; because it sought to serve the ends of affection, centered upon the things which outstrip the proving senses, the things of God and the human soul, religion, philosophy, beauty.

7. THE ARCH OF TRIUMPH

Among the many architectural works of the Romans none was more characteristic than the so-called triumphal arch. Of all the architectural works of Greece and Rome none has exerted more influence on modern times. It is doubtful if any commemorative monument equals the arch of triumph, or the communal arch as some would call it, in its combined fitness and simplicity.[14] This particular form of monument united the elements of arch and order, in a way that has powerfully affected our own design as we shall see. The arch of Titus is a typical and fine example. It consists of a barrel vault carried by massive piers that stand at opposite sides of the road-way which the arch spans. The piers have the characteristic high base. Above this base they rise to a level slightly higher than the crown of the vault. At this level, resting on the piers and the vault, there is an oblong, rectangular mass of masonry called *attic*. The weight of the attic strengthens the structure and adds to the sense of security. The design is one which bespeaks permanence and repose, qualities especially to be desired in such a monument. So much for the actual structure and the relations of its main component parts; perfect exemplification of the Roman method of building.

But the Arch of Titus is decorated and, what is more, its decoration makes what otherwise would be an uninteresting mass an object of beauty and dignity. Corinthian columns, with composite capitals of the Corinthian and Ionic Orders, the first use of the Composite Order, partly bedded in the masonry, an engaged order, are set upon the inner and outer angles of the piers. They rest upon the high base and they carry, likewise engaged, a com-

plete entablature. Thus the arch is framed
in the right lines of columns and entablatures.
The actual vault is emphasized by setting it
somewhat back, thus giving the lower member
of the entablature a heavy projection which, in
turn, makes a deep and effective shadow above
the arch. This decorative but unstructural
use of the orders, though in general foreign to
Greek design, became a universal feature of
Roman. Combining the orders with the arch,
what is called the Roman arch order, was
purely Roman. The effect, singly as with the
Arch of Titus or, in endless succession, as on
the exterior of the Colosseum is always pleasant and often impressive.

The attic is treated with base and crowning
mouldings, a repetition of the idea, but not a
copy of the exact form of the real base, while
its angles are accented by pilasters. These
pilasters continue the idea of a strengthened
angle; always a good point. A close-knit
unity pervades this entire design which was
brought into being for the two-fold purpose of
displaying a commemorative inscription and
carrying aloft a group of commemorative
statuary, usually a *quadriga*. It is rare in
the annals of architecture to find the practical

demands of a problem so completely met at the same time that the requirements of a structural system and a decorative scheme are so consistently respected. But this was to be Roman. It is this that makes Roman architecture, as a whole, and the triumphal arch in particular, so appealing to our age and generation. It is for the example it sets even more than its actual remains that we owe it so great a debt.

There were at least thirty-eight of these arches in Rome alone during the second century, A.D., and they continued to be built in numbers. We know now of nearly five hundred throughout the Roman Empire. Notable among later Roman arches is that of Septimius Severus which dates from the very beginning of the third century, and that of Constantine erected early in the fourth.[15] In modern times the colossal Arc de Triomphe in the Place de l'Étoile, Paris, is the most striking example, but examples, many of them fine as well as large, are to be seen in many of the important cities of Europe, England and America.[16]

8. Theatre,[17] Stadium, Amphitheatre

It was not until Hellenistic times and under Græco-Roman influences that the theatre and the stadium became conspicuous. Theatre building took on distinctive forms in Greek lands during the fourth century B.C., and these forms influenced Roman theatres except where the native dramatic usages, for example a chorus in Greece, no chorus in Italy, were dominating motives in the planning and arrangement of stage and orchestra. The auditorium for musical performances, the Odeum so-called, was closely related to the theatre. The essential features in both cases were concave terraced seats and the back scene behind the stage and orchestra. In the same class is the stadium, a structure for athletic purposes, with seats arranged in tiers on opposite sides of a long narrow space, arena really, with square ends in the Greek and rounded ends in the Roman examples. They were, as now, athletic fields of convenient shape, enclosed with terraced seats. Their construction, then as now, was more a matter of engineering than of architecture. The influence of this class of Roman building upon present-day conditions offers a striking illustration of the purpose of this book. Scarcely a university, not to mention colleges, in America, but is now possessed of a stadium or is planning to build one. The Harvard Stadium is a notable instance.

While the Greeks usually built their theatres in the hollow of a hillside, carrying up the highest tiers of seats in masonry above the crest of the hollow, the Romans early built up the entire structure from the level of a flat site, as the Greeks did at Eretria. In a short time they began to build amphitheatres, a complete circular or elliptical terracing of seats about a circular or elliptical arena. The first stone theatre in Rome was that of Pompey, built in 55 B.C. In quick succession others followed, both in Rome, in other parts of Italy, and in the provinces. The first stone amphitheatre preserved is that at Pompeii, built about 70 B.C. Finally, in 72 A.D., the largest amphitheatre of all, the Colosseum, was undertaken. It has given the idea for many a modern amphitheatre, notably the Yale Bowl. The Colosseum was dedicated, 80 A.D. The topmost story was not added until the second quarter of the third century. In this building we see the most carefully worked out plan and the final splendor of the classic, architectural mind dealing with this peculiarly classic problem, now a problem of our own. The Colosseum is 620 feet on the major axis and 513 feet on the minor. About its elliptical arena there rose three high terraces of seats. Externally the lofty wall was divided into three stories which correspond with the levels of the terraces within. On the ground story eighty entrances led into passages which follow the radii of the ellipse. In the thickness of the walls and terraces most intricate arrangements of concentric and radiating corridors and stairways gave easy access and ready egress to and from all parts of the building. Externally the wall is divided horizontally by entablatures, really string courses, and vertically by engaged columns upon which the entablatures rest. Each column is built into the middle of the face of a pier, the piers being set equidistant from one another around the ellipse of the outer wall. The piers carry an endless succession of arches. Thus the unit of decoration, multiplied beyond counting, is the arch order of the Arch of Titus already described. The continuous sweeping curves of

[133]

the entablatures; the endless repetition of columns; the rhythmical narrowing of the innumerable arches passing from whatever point of view into vanishing perspective; the fact that, because of the elliptical plan, the barrel vaults of every concentric corridor crossed the similar vaults of every radiating corridor, necessitated individual treatment, an irregular form of cross vaults; the fact that a great part of the gigantic mass is built of cut stone, carefully banded with iron clamps set in lead, the interior in marble; the vast seating capacity of 45,000; — all these facts, and many more, prove that the Colosseum was a triumph considered either structurally or decoratively; final proof of the mastery of Roman architecture in the domain of sheer bigness couched in terms of dignity, — in a word, "the grandeur that was Rome."

9. TEMPLES

With unfailing eye for what is practical, and for the most practicable way of attaining ends, the Romans made a modification in temple design which has been followed again and again and still exists in present-day church design. Instead of setting the hall well within the columns of the *peristyle* as did the Greeks, thus sacrificing much space beneath the roof, the Romans moved the wall, on three sides, out to the columns. In other words they retained the open columnar portico across the front, but made the peristyle a matter of engaged columns upon the sides and rear. This gave a hall equal in width to the foundation on which it stood.

The Romans made another change which was destined to affect our architecture. They placed high basements under their temples, thus making the edifice, as a whole, much more conspicuous than the low, broad, stepped foundation made the Greek temple. The high approach which this rendered necessary was provided for by a flight of steps leading up to the portico. These steps were flanked on each side by a wall which was a continuation of the basement forward to the line of the lowest step; arrangement like that of the Pergamum altar.

The best preserved, an extremely beautiful Roman temple, is that at Nîmes in the south of France, the so-called Maison Carrée. It was built at the very beginning of the Christian era. It measures 117 feet by 59 and its base is 11 feet high. The order is Corinthian, the columns being just over 30 feet tall with a diameter of 2 feet and 9 inches. The refinements of this building are remarkable, the delicacy of its curvature of line and surface approaching that of the earlier Greek temples. From this and similar Roman temples modern times have derived such a church as the Madeleine in Paris, Napoleonic temple of victory. Thence, too, were derived many of our earlier city churches, and our idea of the lofty classic portico for many varieties of building set at the top of a flight of steps. The Maison Carrée even gave the idea to Thomas Jefferson for the state capitol of Virginia at Richmond.[18] The United States received the classical style several years before Europe took it up.

10. BATHS

The Roman baths were colossal club houses which included not only every possible convenience and luxury attendant upon the act of bathing, but vast gymnasia for exercise and games, together with halls and rooms, great and small, devoted to the general uses of

readers and loungers. They furnished places
for the meeting of statesmen and their con-
stituents; for poets and philosophers with their
admirers. In them poems and essays were
given to the public for the first time and dis-
cussion of timely topics went on continuously.
As their size was gigantic their arrangements
were highly complex. It is the great central
hall, a vaulted oblong space about which the
various apartments were grouped, that has
especial interest for us today. The most complete remains are those of the Baths of Caracalla, 211–217 A.D. The Roman church of
Santa Maria degli Angeli is the restored hall
of the Baths of Diocletian, 284–305 A.D.; and
other parts have been used to form the National Museum or Museo delle Terme, the
Museum of the Baths.

11. The Basilica of Constantine

The so-called " Basilica " of Constantine
was a great, vaulted hall constructed like the
central halls of the imperial Roman baths.
It may be taken as a type of them. The plan
consisted of a central aisle flanked by narrower
side aisles. The central aisle was 82 feet

across. The side aisles were 50. The central aisle was divided into three square compartments each covered by an elliptical groin vault. A vestibule ran across one end while the other terminated in a semi-circular projection. This projection was covered with a half hemispherical dome. The side aisles were divided into three oblong compartments by cross walls set at right angles to the length of the building and upon the dividing lines of the three square compartments of the central aisle. Each of these was covered with a barrel vault the crown of which ran at right angles to the length of the building. The crowns or intersections of the barrel vaults, which formed the three elliptical groin vaults over the central aisle, were 114 feet above the pavement. The crowns of the barrel vaults over the side aisles were at a considerably lower level. The discrepancy between the height of the central aisle vaults and those of the side aisles left room for a series of windows beneath the central aisle vaults, and above those of the side aisles.

In order to lessen the enormous span of the central aisle vaults, a span of 82 feet, colossal, detached columns were set, one each

against the ends of the walls which divided the
side aisles, — the same walls which supported
the barrel vaults of the side aisles and served
as abutments for the thrusts of the cross
vaults of the central aisle. The groins of the
central aisle vaults come down upon these
columns, each of which projected about 10 feet
on opposite sides of the aisle, thus reducing
the actual vault span to 60 feet. The three
barrel vaults of the north side aisle are still
standing, and masses of projecting masonry,
the beginnings of the groin vaults of the
central aisle, are still securely hanging in mid-
air despite the fact that their supporting
columns have been gone for centuries. These
masses of overhanging masonry bear witness
to the unique quality of Roman concrete, its
strength and durability.

The great hall of the Pennsylvania Railroad
terminal in New York City not only has the
main dispositions of compartment, vaulting
and clerestory but also the details such as
columns for narrowing the vault span, and
vault coffers which the Basilica of Constantine
had. And as the interior of this great modern
railroad station is Roman, so too are the façade
and approaches. Thus one of the chief en-

trances to the richest city of the western world, in the twentieth century, is by way of an edifice so Roman in aspect that it would cause no surprise to Caracalla or Diocletian or to Constantine, were they to return in the flesh and behold it.

That the incomparably impressive character of Roman architecture, due in great measure to the direct and rugged method of its construction, tells upon the mind as beauty is not to be wondered at. Its primary conception of justly proportioned mass, combined with repetition of similar parts, worked out on so colossal a scale as to annul the sense of repetition; the gradual perspective narrowing of the repeated arches, tier on tier of the Colosseum, for example, or the miles on miles of horizon-reaching arches of the aqueducts crossing the Campagna, are attributes which, in themselves, assure beauty. And in many instances where these same aqueducts had to be carried through mountainous country, over rivers and across valleys, often to be used as bridges, they attained a picturesqueness and a charm that is truly beautiful. The Pont du Gard at Nîmes,[19] with its triple ascending arches, 900 feet long and 160 feet high, the

[140]

central arches over the river wider than the
arches of approach, and its imposts ranging
from lower to higher in order to give the necessary slope for the aqueduct, is the finest
existing example, though it was but one of
many examples in its own, and later imperial days. Some of the finest bridges of our
day may claim it proudly as their ancestor.
The spirit of modernism is in it; the key to
the effect which the gigantic engineering-
architectural works of the present day produce upon sane men when they behold use
and dignity permanently joined in one and
the same object; the spirit of the Pont du
Gard, which led Jean Jacques Rousseau to
write: "I walked upon the arches of this
superb construction with a respect that almost
made me shrink from treading on it. Mme. de
Larnage had been very careful to warn me
against the attractions of the young women
of Montpellier, but not against the Pont du
Gard." Those attractions, the attractions of
Roman building considered in the aggregate,
have conquered us as they conquered Rousseau. The Roman stamp impressed upon so
large a part of all our best work is the proof.

VI. DOWN THE AGES

FAILING INVENTION, PHYSICAL DECAY, BIRTH OF THE NEW

1. THE WEST AND MEDIÆVALISM

CERTAIN buildings which typified the actual form, and begot the traditional influence of Greek and Roman architecture have been considered. Though few they are representative of all that was most distinguished for beauty of whole and part, for structure and size. They are, in a way, analogous to the poetry of an epoch; to particular poems which are representative of the whole, and examples of the best, — works of art, extensions of personality into the future, projection and perpetuation of ideas.

This survey has not been attempted in the temper of the historian or critic of architecture. It has sought to lay emphasis on certain architectural attributes and perfections which have been, in one way or another, transmitted to the present time and which, in one way or

another, are actually giving shape to the building of the present day. No work of architecture has been mentioned that is not generally
known. Not a building has been named of
which plans, sections, elevations, details, present condition, and restorations are not to be
found in any one of many easily accessible
books on architecture. This is so, necessarily,
in an essay on " Our Architectural Debt to
Greece and Rome " wherein the appeal is to
lay intelligence rather than to the specialist
in art or archæology, and in an essay where-
from numerous diagrammatic and pictorial illustrations are omitted.

Figuratively speaking, at the time when
Constantine put on the crown, actually, when
he took it to the East, classical architecture
had brought its splendid fruits to ripeness.
It was ready to break up and to scatter the
seed far and wide. This it did. Thereon,
in the West, followed the long period of dis-
integration and germination, variously called
the early Christian centuries, or the beginning of the Dark Ages. The religious, social
and political causes which brought about the
decline of Rome, her architecture as well as
all else that was hers, need only be suggested.

The first thing that happened, a thing that lay at the root of all that followed in the architectural decadence, was the ceasing to build vaults and, in their stead, the general return to timber roofs. For example, such unsurpassed vaulted buildings as the Basilica of Constantine, triumph of engineering skill and acme of dignified design, gave place to structures of the type of the Christian Basilica of St. Paul, and all other Christian basilicas, its kin, with wooden roofs. In these, despite their grave beauty of pillar and mosaic, imposing size and noble vistas, we see the complete change from fire-proof and enduring, in a word, monumental architecture, to everything that is its opposite. Whatever the reasons for this change, the change itself marked a stupendous retrogression; one which fed upon itself in that, as time went on, men more and more forgot what permanent and difficult building meant, for the capital reason that they were called on to do it less and less. Failure, on the part of an individual, a community, or an epoch, to keep up its practice of an art soon becomes a disease which, allowed to go on, ends in death. Architecture between 300 A.D. and 600 A.D. in the West, passes from a live thing to one moribund. The disease that caused this, developed after the age of Constantine, and culminated in the so-called Dark Ages.

Other things also were happening to augment the architectural decadence of the time. For example, a very important one was the growing habit of placing arches on columns, a thing never so much as thought of by the Greeks or Romans of the first two Christian centuries and earlier. But while this meant a seemingly complete break-down of ancient usage, it also meant the origin of one of the loveliest features in all subsequent architecture, the arcade. The Greeks and Romans knew only colonnades, rows of columns connected by lintels. From late imperial times, and from early Christian, the arcade, rows of columns joined together by arches, developed, and the world was the gainer. No word is more dangerous in connection with art than decadence, let us remember, for art, architecture in particular, is like the ever-flowing stream of our generations, the old always bringing the new, and the new always becoming old.

From such buildings as the Basilica of Constantine, in the main, Christianity took the

plan for its first great churches.[20] The broad
central aisle of the former became the nave of
the latter. The side aisles remained as side
aisles. The round projection at the end of
the former became the apse and chancel of
the latter. The colonnaded portico across
the front became the church vestibule. The
clerestory, already described in connection with
the Basilica of Constantine, became an unfailing feature of the larger Christian churches,
and so continues to this moment. Lean-to
roofs took the place of barrel vaults over the
side aisles and a hip roof was substituted
for the elliptical groin or cross vaults above
the nave, the former resting against the outside
wall at a lower level than the eaves of the latter, thus giving space between for windows, the
clerestory. The mediæval cathedrals were
lineal descendants of the Basilica of Constantine by way of the Christian basilica. Further, the so-called Gothic revival in England,
three quarters of a century ago, and our present liking for the beautiful Gothic churches of
Mr. Cram and others alike prove our debt to
Rome. But let it not be forgotten in general
that our debt to the art of the past, specifically
to Greece and Rome, is not like a debt of

money, to be once paid and therewith ended. Rather is it an unpayable debt like that which great men lay upon their country, and wise men on their sons and sons' sons, in that it creates a fresh obligation for each new age; an obligation which is dischargeable only as the new age accepts the model and its spirit, and, by both, is fired to do what is reasonable, beautiful, best and new in the light of present conditions which never can be identical with the conditions of the past, near or remote. The splendid architectural legacy left to the world by Greece and Rome, and transmitted to us by various agents, some of whom have added much to the principal sum, and some of whom have added little or dissipated a part of what was, carries with it architectural responsibility the recognition of which, anywhere and always, is a mark of civilization.

The entablature of Greek and Roman architecture was gradually transformed into the string, or string-course of mediæval building. This came about when, as on the exterior of the Colosseum, the entablature ceased to be the sum of the horizontal members spanning the spaces as, for example, between the columns of a temple front, and became a continuous, boldly-projecting, heavy moulding standing out from the wall; a means of marking off story from story. For instance, the so-called triforium string, or the clerestory string on the inside of a French cathedral, so reasonable as providing a common base for the gallery arches or the windows, and so lovely with patterned carving, is quite unlike its forebear though clearly the descendant of it. On the other hand the Corinthian capital may be said to have held its own, a flaring block, cased in close-encircling foliage, though it suffered total eclipse of beauty as did everything else architectural during the gradual but universal degradation of technique. It fathered all the beautiful, Gothic capitals of northern Europe. But with the capital all likeness to the Corinthian Order, — a possible exception being the base, — or any other order, ends. The Greek order with its column, a thing strictly limited by laws of proportion, makes way for the mediæval pier.

With the passing of the first millennium Western Europe began again to interest itself in the construction of vaulted roofs. The inspiration came mainly from Italy and her ancient capital, but it also came from the remains of the Roman buildings scattered far and wide through what had been the imperial domain. For example, the still-preserved cross-vault of a Roman bath in Paris, now part of the Cluny museum, is but one instance of a model which was not scarce, and upon which the mediæval vault-builder fixed as the starting point for all the miracles which were destined to be performed on his initiative. For the present survey which is of those architectural features only and their spirit that exerted and kept alive the classic influence down the ages, this vault is all-important, — this Roman vault which was the result of applied mathematics, two barrel vaults of semicircular, at any rate of similar curved sections, equal in span and in height, intersecting each other at right angles, exemplified at its best in the Basilica of Constantine. That the architects of the Eastern Roman Empire (their architecture is called Byzantine from the earlier Greek name of Constantinople) treated the cross-vault with a freedom unknown to Rome is a fact of much importance in explaining the origin of mediæval vaulting. To the inspiration and models of Rome, together with the infiltration of Byzantine Greek ideas of modification, ideas which consisted chiefly in discarding rigid mathematical principles and building, so to speak, free-hand, and with lighter materials as against massive concrete, the architects of the Middle Ages, particularly northern France, brought their vitalizing genius. The result was Paris, Amiens, Rheims and all their derivatives, Westminster Abbey, Cologne, Burgos. In the return to the cross-vault idea, a return which culminated in the great departure which we know as mediæval vaulting, and in the demand for monumental construction, which was the reason why the mind of the Middle Ages turned to the cross-vault, are included the main items of the incalculable debt which we have to acknowledge indirectly to the Middle Ages and directly to Greece and Rome.

2. THE EAST AND MEDIÆVALISM

For our needs an even briefer survey of the architectural movement in the Eastern Empire will suffice. The first fact to be noted is that the East never let go of the idea of the dome, an idea which had its origin there, but which was inspired to new triumphs of realization by the dome of the Pantheon. The Byzantine architects of Justinian were destined to raise over the Church of Holy Wisdom in Constantinople a dome of unsurpassed beauty and majesty. In size it was not equal to the dome of the Pantheon. For ease of construction, and consequent cost, it was superior. In that it showed how a round dome can be set, securely and gracefully, over a square space, and on four piers, a thing unknown to the Romans, it was epochal. To the Romans a dome necessarily meant a circular room and a continuous, circular, supporting wall. The East freed dome builders from this hampering restriction. From the East, Constantinople, this discovery passed to Italy, finding embodiment at the hands of Theodoric in Ravenna, of Charlemagne in Aix-la-Chapelle, and finally appearing at St. Mark's in Venice. It remains true however that the Middle Ages in the West did not greatly concern themselves with the dome. They left it to the Renaissance, and so will we, remembering the while that Rome, the West, gave the first great example while Constantinople, the East, of Greek origin, gave that freedom which was necessary before the Roman example and its tradition could be treated as the Renaissance was to treat them through Michelangelo, in the church of St. Peter's, and as we, his followers, in the dome of our Capitol in Washington.

In Rome a cross-vault meant a square plan or space beneath. The idea of building such vaults over spaces longer than they were wide, — again the expression ' free-hand building ' is descriptive, — and of relinquishing strict mathematical procedure and using light materials instead of massive concrete, was of Byzantine Greek origin. From the East this idea found its way *via* North Italy to Northern Europe, to France in particular, in the earliest Middle Age. This fresh conception of the cross-vault, together with the Roman example of the round arch, were the two chief influences which led the inventive architectural mind and capable hands of the Lombards and the French to create the so-called Romanesque style. Of it Rome was the inspirer; Constantinople the quickener. It is to this Romanesque architecture, mothered and fathered by West and East, that we in this country are indebted for such fine buildings as Trinity Church in Boston, and the Harvard Law School, the work of Richardson, and for the good work of his many followers. The causes and effects of the Greek and Roman influences upon Mediæ-val builders sometimes conscious of them, more often not, may be described in a few words of Emerson written of an utterly different subject: "As wind and rain play into one another's hands in nature, so do human minds."

Then, it seems to have been in the twinkling of an eye, but really was not, the Gothic style appeared. The low, round arch gave way to the high pointed. The heavy made place for the light. A system of building, the Roman-esque, which depended in large measure upon inert mass, as did its forebears of Greece, Rome and Constantinople, disappeared, — in the sense of being no longer used, — from the face of Europe, and its place was taken by the Gothic system which meant the balancing and opposing of thrust to thrust, an active system, even a restless one, structurally speaking. It was as logical as anything the Greeks or the Romans produced. It was exquisite in the Greek sense, and complex in the Roman. Its towers and spires rose into heaven. But its admiration for the vast was a legacy from Rome. Without the forerunning classical in-

fluences, and their transmitters, Gothic could
not have been. Had it incorporated classical
reasonableness and restraint its vogue would
not so easily have lapsed, or its beauty
crumbled as was actually the case when in
1574 the spire of Beauvais fell and, figuratively, not to add dramatically, the way for
the return to antiquity was made straight, so
that the Renaissance, already on foot in Florence, could easily carry all before it as it
marched to every corner of Europe, and
crossed the English Channel. But that an
imaginative understanding, the only true understanding where art is concerned, of Roman
grandeur and Greek beauty, call it similar
feeling for sanity of structure and for loveliness of detail if you like, did not brood over
the mediæval builders' mind is impossible to
disprove and impossible not to believe. True,
Gothic masons knew no more of Greek buildings than did Gothic scholars of Greek letters
at first hand. But the light of the Greek spirit
shone upon them equally, dim and many times
refracted though it was. That spirit is in
Gothic church and statue as it is in the
consummate edifice of mediæval words, the
Divine Comedy, wherein its author, who calls

Rome "revered," almost piously describes Athens as "the city whence shines forth all knowledge."

3. The Renaissance

And buried learning rose, redeem'd to a new morn.

This line of Byron's which describes Florence as the birth-place of the Renaissance, though literally true must also be taken as typical of the half-truth which rests on the double assumption that there was no real learning there before the Renaissance, and that the Gothic learning of the north, preëminently of France, had no part in bringing about the Renaisssance. What has been said, in respect to Gothic, specifically of the fall of the spire of Beauvais, about clearing the way for the Renaissance should not be taken too literally. Byron says *buried* learning, and *means* buried; Greek and Roman. He could never have forgotten the glorious, mediæval learning of Florence, typified by all the arts, and incarnate in the *Divine Comedy*, that bulwark of the classics which is the sole, adequate laud yet sung to Virgil, and the unparalleled begetter of enthusiasm and respect for things Greek as well as Roman. Neither can any who are, as we, interested in that particular form of learning which finds expression in architecture, keep even moderate faith with facts and not recognize in the mediæval dome of the Baptistery of Florence the prototype of that vast, first work of the Renaissance, Brunelleschi's dome of the Cathedral close by, nor in this same vast work fail to see mediæval French, architectural influence, however remote. It is imperative to bear in mind that when Brunelleschi went to Rome in 1403 to study ancient architecture, especially the dome of the Pantheon, the unfinished cathedral of his native city was calling for a dome such as had not been thought of since imperial Roman times. Further, to remember, that from his boyhood in Florence he had been familiar with a dome of eight sides, and pointed section, the broken arch, *arc brisé,* of French Gothic, for such was the dome of the eleventh century Baptistery. Finally, not to forget that the dome which he did build for the Florentine cathedral is octagonal and has a pointed section, which proclaims, indubitably, the influence of mediæval French architecture whether directly, or through the baptistery, indirectly, upon Brunelleschi.

The figure which describes Dante as having bridged the chasm between the Middle Ages and the Renaissance may be true, but the verb link or bind is the verb to describe truthfully what Brunelleschi did to the Middle Ages and the Renaissance, so far as architecture is concerned. Brunelleschi was the father of Renaissance architecture. The light of the future and the light of the past both illumined his genius.

The aim of the builders of the Renaissance was to reproduce the architecture of Rome, but they did not at first know it sufficiently well to be able to do this. The happy result was, room left for play of imagination. The magnificent scale on which the Romans worked, and their perfect structural solutions of very difficult building-problems constitute the crowning glory of their architecture. Brunelleschi sensed this, and was inspired accordingly, though he worked independently of any specific Roman model, whether he was building his great dome or the famous little chapel of the Pazzi family.

As the Renaissance moved forward, that extraordinary man, Alberti, born 1404, introduced what may be called architectural scholarship, connoisseurial writing. This led in some degree to the neglect of the architecture of structural cause and effect, the real architecture always. With him may be said to have begun the unending series of treatises on architecture, the foundation for all of which was the Latin treatise by Vitruvius who probably died before the first Christian century opened. At all events he did not know imperial Roman architecture, and he was in the main unfamiliar with Greek. His position is due mainly to the fact that by fortunate chance his book has survived. Because of the time in which he wrote he came to be regarded almost with pious awe; as an absolute authority. This authority still clings to his name.

Later than Alberti, Peruzzi, (born 1480), as the result of his classical researches and an unusual combination of strength and fineness of mind, bestowed on architecture, in a manner little short of marvelous, qualities akin to those of the Greek itself, — in a word, refinement, at once virile and delicate. He knew classical instances as Alberti did not, and he used them with an intellectual freedom and restraint that made his design, and his writing,

[158]

almost Greek, yet not Greek at all. Exquisite detail of classical origin he used as means for emphasizing scale. The Massimi Palace in Rome is unsurpassed, and has been seldom equalled in this respect. It is architecture which never could have been but for its far-distant, classical ancestor, yet it is in no sense the architecture of an archæologist or a theorist, however learned. It is the architecture of a builder who has bestowed the charm of appropriate ornament upon every fundamental feature of his construction.

Wherever the eye of thought turns, the Italian Renaissance has left church fronts from Brunelleschi's day and the Pazzi Chapel, Alberti's Sant' Andrea in Mantua and San Francesco in Rimini, down to Maderna's front of St. Peter's in Rome, all of which are frankly and splendidly adapted from imperial Roman design. The Colossal Order, an order rising through several stories, was the invention of Palladio, yet the order itself was Roman, and Greek before it was Roman. Temple fronts and triumphal arches applied to new uses came into existence everywhere. The same is true of palaces from the Rucellai, fifteenth century Florentine, Alberti's, to the Farnese in Rome, by San Gallo the younger and Michelangelo. A glance at the court-yard of the Farnese recalls the exterior of the Colosseum with its orders superimposed, story on story. Our modern office buildings and shops very frequently are derived from these. Any fine business district in any large American city declares the fact over and over.

Such interior arcades as separate the broad from the side aisles in Brunelleschi's church of San Lorenzo in Florence are from the age of Diocletian. They have come down to us and are to be seen in many a church in this country. But despite all the turning back of the Italian Renaissance to classical models, it developed a masterly habit of using its models; a habit which amounted to actual genius at the hands of the best men. From the thoroughly classical, — yet unlike anything Greece or Rome ever produced, — beautiful, small, circular church of San Pietro in Montorio by Bramante, in Rome, on to that culminating and transcendent work of Michelangelo, the dome of St. Peter's, the classical impress, and the impress of the age of revived classicism are to be recognized. Neither of these buildings, so commanding in presence and antipodal in size, nor hundreds more, could have been, — any more than the architectural tradition which they embodied, — but for the architectural fragments and partial ruins of ancient Rome, among which they rose to the " new morn." And had not the Renaissance, figuratively, handed on the torch, Sir Christopher Wren would never have built St. Paul's in London, and we should not have the Capitol in Washington.

The same is true of palace fronts, the Louvre in Paris, Whitehall in London, the City Hall in Philadelphia. Orders, entablatures, arches, domes — these were the vocabulary and the rhetoric of the language of architecture in Greece and Rome. Changed, corrupted, adapted, given new life, taken possession of unintelligently and bodily, or used as points of departure, — such was the procedure of the Renaissance in relation to the classical.

The painters of Italy, also, had an important part in handing down the facts and the tradition of classical architecture, as well as the writer-architects. Mantegna, Perugino, Raphael and many more set their subjects in almost archæologically correct surroundings of classical architecture, or created lovely adaptations of it. The sense of beauty which they derived from it, and the power of beauty with which they endowed it, cannot be passed over lightly when one reflects upon the influence which Italian painting exerted on its own people in its own day, and has ever since, and now exerts on all people. Their canvases soon began to travel and have never ceased to do so. They carried ideas and knowledge, and the germs of both, in a manner analogous to the books of Serlio, Palladio, Vignola and San Gallo. It is but necessary to name Mantegna's " Triumph of Cæsar," Perugino's " Marriage of the Virgin," Raphael's " School of Athens," or Titian's " Presentation of the Virgin," to call to mind splendid architecture of strictly classical type, or ' arranged,' to borrow a term from the musicians. The common purpose of artists in the widest sense, one and all, sometimes consciously, sometimes unconsciously, was to " awake the dead." They did not do it, but, at best, they did a far better thing. They gave life to a new and beautiful creature who forthwith went to all parts of the European continent, to Britain, and, finally, to America.

4. BEYOND THE ALPS AND THE ENGLISH CHANNEL

" The descent of poetry has been from Greece to Italy, and from Italy to England," to quote Gray; this is paralleled by the descent of architecture, France having the right to claim a place as an important, collateral connection in this figurative genealogy of art. When the Renaissance movement first made itself felt in France, it did so by applying classical detail to Gothic structure. This gave the world that fascinating transitional style called by the name of Francis First because it was typical of the work of his reign. For example, the Château of Chambord. Among churches, Saint Eustache in Paris is a notable instance. Meantime, increasingly, direct importations of the architectural style of Renaissance Italy came to be the habit. Vignola, one of the most important writer-architects, an authority on the orders, along with other Italian designers, worked at Fontainebleau, while Serlio, another Italian architect and author, had much to do with rebuilding the Louvre, though Lescot was officially its architect at this period, 1544. Louis Fourteenth's grandiose classicism at

Versailles must be mentioned, together with the eighteenth century domes of the Invalides and the Panthéon, and that classic temple, the Madeleine in Paris, each of which, along with many more, is significant in tracing the descending course of Greek and Roman influence as it approaches our own day.

In England as in France, the Renaissance first effected a transitional style of architecture and then took controlling hold. The change had begun to show before the death of Elizabeth, 1603, but not until the time of James the First, was there an English architect who gained merited fame by building in the Renaissance manner. This was Inigo Jones. He studied in Italy and designed many English buildings in the manner of Palladio, notably the Palace of Whitehall for Charles the First. But, towering above all others was Sir Christopher Wren who, in the period of fifty years following the Fire of 1666, clothed London in classical buildings, the Royal Exchange, innumerable private structures, half a hundred churches and St. Paul's Cathedral. Greek and Roman temple fronts, the orders, pure, varied according to the usage of the Renaissance, or treated freely by himself; round arches,

framed in the right lines of column and lintel,
niches and balustrades, are everywhere to be
seen in Sir Christopher's buildings, at Oxford and Cambridge not less than in London.
Their intrinsic charm, coupled with the classical sanction, and Wren's authority, soon made
them at home wherever the English tongue
was spoken. The dome of St. Paul's set the
last seal on his authority just as St. Peter's
dome did upon the authority of Michelangelo.

The eighteenth century numbers a long list
of conspicuous followers of Wren, all clas-
sicists, among whom were the famous brothers
Adam, who built the Adelphi, and Dance, who
built the Mansion House, both in London.
This time too saw rise many of the great
country houses of England in the classical,
Renaissance style, the manner of Palladio
being dominant. The greater part of this
work was pompous like that of the corresponding epoch across the Channel. But it was
Roman, by way of Italian Renaissance.

In 1762 something occurred which almost
brought about a revolution in architectural
taste. This was the publication of the *Antiquities of Athens* by Stuart and Revett, a
book the text and pictures of which turned

[165]

architectural thought to the refinements, they would have said the purities, of Greek architecture, and away from Roman. By 1800 there was an overwhelming desire to have every building, and all architectural detail, absolutely Greek. This, which was to attempt the impossible, did nevertheless bring about much that was finely restrained, though often cold.

This is the place to speak of the etched work of Piranesi,[21] the portraitist *par excellence* of the ruins of Rome. It is unique in quality and of colossal extent, including, as it does, more than a thousand pictures of Roman architecture as it looked in the middle of the eighteenth century. Each picture is faithful to literal fact, as well as poetically truthful to the spirit of past magnificence. Sir William Chambers, architect of Somerset House in London, knew Piranesi in Rome between 1747 and 1755. To Chambers, in no small degree, was due the introduction of Piranesi's work to Englishmen upon whom it exerted great, as well as immediate, influence, because it spread broadcast among the patrons of architecture a knowledge of Roman architecture and therewith set them on fire to copy it. No man of fashion could be without Piranesi's depictions, and such is their grandeur, many would say, pomposity, that few men could, or can, withstand their attractions. To the name of Chambers should be added the names of George Dance, designer of Old Newgate Prison, and Dance's pupil, John Soane, later Sir John, who built the Bank of England, and the brothers Adam, who inaugurated the Classical style in Edinburgh. Further, the English eighteenth-century custom of traveling abroad, making the grand tour as it was called, especially of Italy, resulted in bringing home to England many sets of Piranesi. This meant not only ancient Roman buildings, but Renaissance architecture, based on Roman, as well. The story of the descent of classical architecture down the ages may not omit Piranesi's unparalleled power as the linear interpreter of Roman grandeur. His fascination is shown nowhere better than in that conception of his *Opere Varie*, 1750, in which, surrounded by the circular wall of the Pantheon, and beneath its very dome, he leads us up to its floor by interminable curving ramps of urned and balustraded stairs, through mighty, statue-capped colonnades; a conception which beggars credibility but portrays Rome truthfully. In his actual transcripts of

Roman ruins, and in such imaginative compositions as I have just referred to, Piranesi gives warrant for the words of Sir Reginald Blomfield when he says that Roman architecture is " forever memorable in the splendid courage of its construction, in its capacity for ordered thought, dealing with vast conceptions. It is because of its superb resource, of its masterful method of conquering any and every problem set it that Roman architecture remains the greatest and most profitable study for the serious architect." Against this we may set the statement of Professor A. Kingsley Porter: " Of all historic styles it (the Roman) presents the closest analogies with the architecture of the nineteenth century in America. It is also, of all historic styles, evidently the least illustrative, the most material." And, says the same high authority, years later: " I still see in Roman architecture, as I did a decade ago, emptiness, pomposity, vulgarity." Finally, " Inspired by the beauty of the ruins, a Piranesi might imagine Roman art fired with an originality, a joyousness, which the Romans never knew. Many architects, notably our own Thomas Jefferson, have done precisely this. Thus the shade of Rome was shrouded

[168]

with phantom glory." " Phantom glory" is
a singularly happy phrase because it describes
completely the immeasurable influence,
whether for good or evil, which the ghost of
Rome exerts upon the body of the present.

5. BEYOND THE ATLANTIC. COLONIAL ARCHI-
TECTURE TODAY, BUT NOT THE END

In America the colonists followed, as closely
as conditions would allow, the English Renaissance and Classical styles of building; wood
to a great extent taking the place of stone.
After the Revolution we continued to build in
the same manner, Colonial by a misnomer, it
is called. The ample, dignified, serene porticoes, Doric, Ionic, Corinthian, of dwelling
houses and public buildings which all along
the Atlantic seaboard have come down in
generous number are full of charm. Palladio's
colossal order, together with many a minor
detail of the Italian Renaissance, *via* England,
came direct to our shores. So too, did the
French version of the Renaissance. George
Washington had Major L'Enfant lay out plans
for the city that was to be our capital, while
the oldest part of the Capitol itself is in the

austerely classical style of design which was
the then French vogue, as well as English.
A little later, Thomas Jefferson reinforced the
tradition of American Classicism in his building for the University of Virginia, and everywhere in his fine work one can see how he
strove to adapt and emulate the nobility of
Roman architecture as he conceived it, through
his study of treatises, and pictures. Thus
were the foundations of our architecture, and
its continuance through many years, classical.
First Roman, then Greek, the inspiration and
the pattern were received in the main from
England, in part from France, from those who
had received the legacy from renascent Italy,
the heir direct of Rome and Greece. And yet,
despite the Romanesque and Gothic revival
which has given us numerous fine and lovely
structures, especially since the dawn of the
twentieth century, the dominant note in
American architecture today is classic. Witness our state capitols, such as that of Providence, Rhode Island; many of our great com-
mercial structures, the Park Row Building,
New York, or the Gas Building, Chicago;
many of our ephemeral structures, often very
beautiful, the Fair buildings in Chicago or in

San Francisco; out-door theatres, that of the University of California or that of the University of Virginia;[22] public libraries, that of New York City; Art Museums, those in Boston, and New York; Hall of Records, New York; memorials, the Allegheny County Soldiers' Memorial in Pittsburgh. The number of similar buildings is legion.[23] Their testimony is one. For by far the larger part of our important approximations to architectural perfection, and even for our architectural imperfections, we, like Britain and the Continent, are indebted directly and indirectly to Greece and Rome. If it be true that " Except for the blind forces of nature, nothing moves in this world which is not Greek in its origin," it is also true that Rome interpreted the architecture of Greece in such a way as to make it suitable for the uses of this twentieth Christian century.

NOTES AND BIBLIOGRAPHY

NOTES

1. A. S Hartwick in his *Drawing*, London, 1921, says: "Finally there remains one more form of beauty, . . . namely, beauty of craftmanship and execution. I hold it safe to say that it is impossible to express the finest emotion in art without superlative command of craft or technique."

2. The twenty-four huge, Corinthian columns of the New York Hall of Records are the largest monoliths in the world.

3. The so-called Ionic frieze seems often to have been omitted in the buildings of Asia Minor.

4. On the origin of the Corinthian Order, cf. the very interesting article of T. Homolle, " L'Origine du Chapiteau Corinthien," *Revue Archéologique*, IV. 17 ff. (1916). Some important material has recently been published by Margaret Gütschow, " Untersuchungen zum korinthischen Kapitell," *Jahrbuch des deutschen archäologischen Instituts*, XXXVI. 44 ff. (1921). The fragments of the Corinthian capital from the temple at Bassae, which Dinsmoor dates as early as 450 but others with more correctness about 420 B.C., are here discussed. For the Corinthian Order in general cf. E. Weigand, *Die Vorgeschichte des korinthischen Kapitells*, Würzburg, 1920.

5. Whether Mr. Hambidge, in his important and interesting writings, has dealt a death-blow to this view of our subject remains for time to prove.

6. On the Parthenon cf. M. Collignon, *Le Parthénon*, 2 vols., Paris, 1912–1914; M. Schede, *Die Burg von Athen*, Berlin, 1922; A. H. Smith, *British Museum. The Sculptures of the Parthenon*, London, 1910; *Art and Archaeology*, IV. 7–46 (1916). For the earlier Parthenon, cf.

B. H. Hill, *American Journal of Archaeology,* XVI. 535 ff. (1912).

7. For the Nashville Parthenon cf. *Art and Archaeology,* I. 256 (1915); XII. 75 ff. (1912). For the Bavarian adaptation near Ratisbon (Regensburg), the Walhalla, the German Temple of Fame, cf. *Art and Archaeology,* II. 60 (1915). The statement in the *Encyclopedia Brittanica* that Girard College in Philadelphia is " the most perfect copy of the Parthenon in existence " is exaggerated. It is a parody and a poor adaptation. The architect was thinking of the Parthenon and his architecture was influenced by the Parthenon, but there are countless characteristics in the Parthenon which are not suggested in Girard College.

8. This building was long ago pulled down and its marbles built into a Turkish fortress on the Acropolis. It was rebuilt from the rescued parts and material about eighty years ago. Cf. C. H. Weller, *Athens and its Monuments,* New York, 1913, 240 ff.

9. For the dating of the sixteen extant columns in the time of Hadrian, cf. A. D. Fraser, *The Art Bulletin,* IV. 5 ff. (1921).

10. Cf. *Art and Archaeology,* V. 13 ff. (1917); D. G. Hogarth, *Excavations at Ephesus, the Archaic Artemisia,* London, 1908; H. C. Butler, " The Elevated Columns at Sardis and the Sculptured Pedestals from Ephesus," in *Anatolian Studies,* Manchester, 1923, pp. 51–57.

11. For the most recent account of the temple at Didyma, cf. *Art and Archaeology,* IX. 187 ff. (1920). In *ibid.* 171 ff. is also a description of the great Ionic temple of Artemis at Sardis excavated by the Americans. Cf. H. C. Butler, *Sardis,* I and II (1922 and 1923), Leyden.

12. For the different reconstructions of the Mausoleum cf. W. B. Dinsmoor, *American Journal of Archaeology,* XII. 3 ff. and 141 ff. (1908). For a popular article cf. *Art and Archaeology,* V. 137 ff. (1917).

13. For a popular article on " Ephesus and Pergamum " cf. D. M. Robinson, *Art and Archaeology,* IX. 157 ff. (1920). Cf. also E. Pontremoli and M. Collignon, *Pergame,* 1900;

Altertümer von Pergamon published by the Königliche Museen zu Berlin; vol. III, 2, *Die Friese des grossen Altars,* 1910.

14. Cf. C. D. Curtis, "Roman Monumental Arches," *Supplementary Papers of the American School of Classical Studies in Rome,* II. 26 ff. (1908). Curtis and Frothingham speak of communal arches. The phrase "triumphal arch" was not used till late and then only in two or three African inscriptions.

15. A. L. Frothingham thinks that the arch of Constantine is earlier (time of Aurelian 273 or Probus 279 A.D.) and that the sculptures were taken from an arch of Lucius Verus and Marcus Aurelius and from another arch of Marcus Aurelius alone (second century A.D.); cf. *American Journal of Archaeology,* XVI. 368 ff. (1912); XVII. 487 ff. (1913); XIX. 1 ff. (1915).

16. An arch of victory was recently erected, after the great war, on Fifth Avenue, New York, which imitated the Roman arch at Orange, but it has since been removed.

17. Another volume in this *Series* will discuss the Theatre and its development.

18. Cf. Fiske Kimball, "Thomas Jefferson and the Origins of the Classical Revival in America," *Art and Archaeology,* I. 219 ff. (1915).

19. Cf. F. B. Tarbell, *Art and Archaeology,* II. 44 ff. (1915).

20. There are instances in which the private basilica, a large house or palace, was devoted by its owner to Christian uses. In almost all cases, however, the Christian basilica was built new for its sacred purpose.

21. Cf. A. Samuel, *Piranesi,* London, 1910; R. V. D. Mogoffin, *Art and Archaeology,* VI. 25 ff. (1917).

22. Cf. also "The Greek Theatre at Bloomfield Hills, Mich.," *Art and Archaeology,* V. 173 ff. (1917); "The Roman Theatre," *ibid.* I. 137 ff., 187 ff. (1915). For the Greek amphitheatre at the Univ. of Va., cf. *New York Times Book Review and Magazine,* Jan. 23, 1921, p. 17.

23. Cf. "Modern Masterpieces of Classical Architecture," "Lincoln Memorial," *Art and Archaeology,* I. 39

(1914); "Monument to Victor Emmanuel," *ibid.* I. 81
(1914); "The Temple of the Scottish Rite," *ibid.* I. 130
(1914); "Field Museum of Natural History," *ibid.* I. 208
(1915); "Nashville Parthenon," *ibid.* I. 256 (1915); "The
Walhalla," *ibid.* II. 60 (1915); "The Arlington Amphitheatre," Washington, *ibid.* III. 231 (1916).

BIBLIOGRAPHY

ADAMS, H., *Mont-Saint-Michel and Chartres*. Boston, 1913.

ANDERSON, W. J., *The Architecture of the Renaissance in Italy*. London, 1909.

ANDERSON, W. J., and SPIERS, R. P., *The Architecture of Greece and Rome*.[3] London, 1923.

BLOMFIELD, SIR R. T., *A History of French Architecture, from the reign of Charles VIII till the death of Mazarin*. 2 vols. London, 1911.

BLOMFIELD, SIR R. T., *A History of Renaissance Architecture in England, 1500–1800*. 2 vols. London, 1897.

BLOMFIELD, SIR R. T., *The Mistress Art*. London, 1908.

BLOMFIELD, SIR. R. T., " Architecture," in *The Legacy of Greece* (edited by R. W. Livingstone). Oxford, 1921.

BROOKS, A. M., *Architecture and the Allied Arts*. Indianapolis, 1914.

BROOKS, A. M., *Great Artists and Their Works by Great Authors*. Boston, 1919.

BROWN, G. B., *The Fine Arts*. New York, 1916.

BUTLER, H. C., *Story of Athens*. New York, 1902.

CAFFIN, I., *How to Study Architecture*. New York, 1917.

CAGNAT, R. L. V., ET CHAPOT, V., *Manuel d'Archéologie Romaine*. Vols. 1–2. Paris, 1916–1920.

CARPENTER, R., *The Esthetic Basis of Greek Art*. New York, 1921.

CHOISY, A., *Histoire de l'Architecture*. 2 vols. Paris, 1899.

COLVIN, SIR SIDNEY, *Memories and Notes of persons and places*. New York, 1921.

CRAM, R. A., *The Ministry of Art*. Boston, 1914.

CRAM, R. A., *The Substance of Gothic*. Boston, 1917.

CUMMINGS, C. A., *A History of Architecture in Italy*

[179]

from the time of Constantine to the dawn of the Renaissance. 2 vols. Boston, 1901.

D'OOGE, M. L., *The Acropolis of Athens.* New York and London, 1908.

DURM, J., *Baukunst der Renaissance in Italien.* Stuttgart, 1903.

DURM, J., *Handbuch der Architektur.* Stuttgart, 1881–1905.

ESPOUY, H. d', *Monuments Antiques.* Vols. 1–3. Paris, 1896–1912.

FAURE, E., *History of Art.* Vol. 1, 2. New York, 1921.

FERGUSSON, JAMES, *A History of Architecture* (New edition, edited by R. H. Spiers. 2 vols.). New York, 1907.

FOWLER, H. N., and WHEELER, J. R., *A Handbook of Greek Archaeology.* New York, 1909.

FRAZER, SIR J. G., *Pausanias's Description of Greece.* 6 vols. Reprinted, London, 1914.

FROTHINGHAM, A. L., *Roman Cities in Italy and Dalmatia.* New York, 1910.

GARDNER, E. A., *Ancient Athens.* New York and London, 1902.

GOODYEAR, W. H., *Greek Refinements.* New Haven, 1912.

HAMBIDGE, J., *Dynamic Symmetry.* New Haven, 1920.

HAMLIN, A. D. F., *A Text-book of the History of Architecture.* New York, 1909.

HAMLIN, A. D. F., *History of Ornament.* New York, 1916.

HAVERFIELD, F., *Ancient Town Planning.* Oxford, 1913.

JACKSON, SIR T. G., *Byzantine and Romanesque Architecture.* 2 vols. Cambridge, England, 1913.

JACKSON, SIR T. G., *Gothic Architecture.* Cambridge, England, 1915.

KIMBALL, S. F., *Thomas Jefferson, Architect.* Boston, 1916.

KIMBALL, S. F., and EDGELL, G. H., *A History of Architecture.* New York and London, 1918.

LEROUX, G., *Les Origines de l'Édifice Hypostyle.* Paris, 1913.

LONGFELLOW, W. P. P., *A Cyclopaedia of Works of*

Architecture in Italy, Greece and the Levant. New York, 1895.

LONGFELLOW, W. P. P., *The Column and the Arch.* New York, 1899.

MARQUAND, A., *Greek Architecture.* New York, 1909.

MOORE, C. H., *Character of Renaissance Architecture.* London and New York, 1905.

MOORE, C. H., *Development and Character of Gothic Architecture.* London and New York, 1899.

PERROT, G., ET CHIPIEZ, C., *Histoire de l'Art dans l'Antiquité.* 10 vols. Paris, 1882–1914.

PLATNER, S. B., *The Topography and Monuments of Ancient Rome.*[2] Boston, 1911.

PONTREMOLI, E., ET COLLIGNON, M., *Pergame, restauration et description des monuments de l'Acropole.* Paris, 1900.

PORTER, A. K., *Beyond Architecture.* Boston, 1918.

PORTER, A. K., *Lombard Architecture.* 4 vols. New Haven, 1915–17.

PORTER, A. K., *Mediaeval Architecture.* 2 vols. New York, 1909.

RUSHFORTH, G. McN., "Architecture and Art," in *The Legacy of Rome* (edited by Cyril Bailey). Oxford, 1923.

SIMPSON, F. M., *History of Architectural Development.* London and New York, 1905–1911.

STATHAM, H. H., *A Short Critical History of Architecture.* London and New York, 1912.

STATHAM, H. H., *Architecture for General Readers.* New York, 1896.

STOBART, J. C., *The Grandeur that was Rome.*[2] London, 1920.

STURGIS, R., *A Dictionary of Architecture and Building.* New York and London, 1901–02.

SYMONDS, J. A., *Renaissance in Italy: The Fine Arts.* New York, 1908.

TARBELL, F. B., *A History of Greek Art.* New York, 1896.

VIOLLET-LE-DUC, E. E., *Discourses on Architecture* (Translation, with introduction, by H. Van Brunt). Boston, 1875.

WALKER, C. H., CRAM, R. A., MAGONIGLE, H. V. B., and CRET, PAUL P., *The Significance of the Fine Arts* (Chapters on *Architecture*). Boston, 1923.

WALTERS, H. B., *The Art of the Romans.* London and New York, 1922.

WARREN, H. L., *The Foundations of Classic Architecture.* New York, 1919.

WATERHOUSE, P. L., *The Story of the Art of Building.* New York, 1903.

PERIODICALS

American Journal of Archaeology, the Journal of the Archaeological Institute of America, Concord, N. H.

The Architectural Review, Boston.

Art and Archaeology, Baltimore and Washington.

The Journal of the American Institute of Architects, Harrisburg and Washington.

For a full bibliography see *The Art Bulletin,* vol. III. no. 1. An illustrated quarterly published by the College Art Association of America, Providence.

INDEX

INDEX

INDEX

[189]

Our Debt to Greece and Rome

AUTHORS AND TITLES

HOMER. *John A. Scott.*

SAPPHO. *David M. Robinson.*

EURIPIDES. *F. L. Lucas.*

ARISTOPHANES. *Louis E. Lord.*

DEMOSTHENES. *Charles D. Adams.*

THE POETICS OF ARISTOTLE. *Lane Cooper.*

GREEK RHETORIC AND LITERARY CRITICISM. *W. Rhys Roberts.*

LUCIAN. *Francis G. Allinson.*

CICERO AND HIS INFLUENCE. *John C. Rolfe.*

CATULLUS. *Karl P. Harrington.*

LUCRETIUS AND HIS INFLUENCE. *George Depue Hadzsits.*

OVID. *Edward Kennard Rand.*

HORACE. *Grant Showerman.*

VIRGIL. *John William Mackail.*

SENECA THE PHILOSOPHER. *Richard Mott Gummere.*

APULEIUS. *Elizabeth Hazelton Haight.*

MARTIAL. *Paul Nixon.*

PLATONISM. *Alfred Edward Taylor.*

ARISTOTELIANISM. *John L. Stocks.*

STOICISM. *Robert Mark Wenley.*

LANGUAGE AND PHILOLOGY. *Roland G. Kent.*

AUTHORS AND TITLES

AESCHYLUS AND SOPHOCLES. *J. T. Sheppard.*

GREEK RELIGION. *Walter Woodburn Hyde.*

SURVIVALS OF ROMAN RELIGION. *Gordon J. Laing.*

MYTHOLOGY. *Jane Ellen Harrison.*

ANCIENT BELIEFS IN THE IMMORTALITY OF THE SOUL. *Clifford H. Moore.*

STAGE ANTIQUITIES. *James Turney Allen.*

PLAUTUS AND TERENCE. *Gilbert Norwood.*

ROMAN POLITICS. *Frank Frost Abbott.*

PSYCHOLOGY, ANCIENT AND MODERN. *G. S. Brett.*

ANCIENT AND MODERN ROME. *Rodolfo Lanciani.*

WARFARE BY LAND AND SEA. *Eugene S. McCartney.*

THE GREEK FATHERS. *James Marshall Campbell.*

GREEK BIOLOGY AND MEDICINE. *Henry Osborn Taylor.*

MATHEMATICS. *David Eugene Smith.*

LOVE OF NATURE AMONG THE GREEKS AND ROMANS. *H. R. Fairclough.*

ANCIENT WRITING AND ITS INFLUENCE. *B. L. Ullman.*

GREEK ART. *Arthur Fairbanks.*

ARCHITECTURE. *Alfred M. Brooks.*

ENGINEERING. *Alexander P. Gest.*

MODERN TRAITS IN OLD GREEK LIFE. *Charles Burton Gulick.*

ROMAN PRIVATE LIFE. *Walton Brooks McDaniel.*

GREEK AND ROMAN FOLKLORE. *William Reginald Halliday.*

ANCIENT EDUCATION. *J. F. Dobson.*

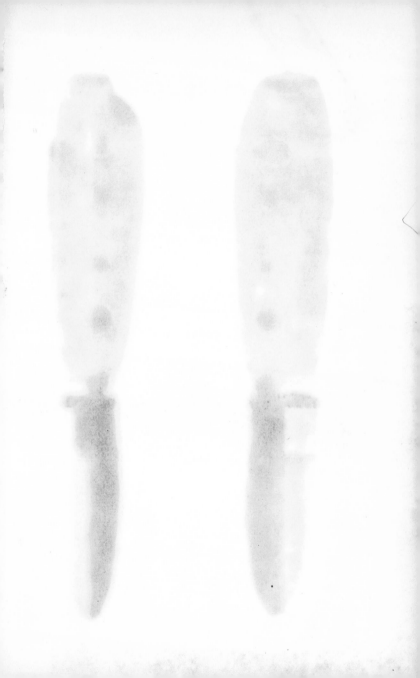

46674

NA
260
B7

BROOKS, ALFRED
    ARCHITECTURE.

DATE DUE	
OCT 12 1997	
NOV 13 1998	
NOV 14 1998	
NOV 19 2003	
DEC 12 2003	
MAY 07 2004	
APR 13 2005	

Perials Library
Colby-Sawyer College
New London, New Hampshire

GAYLORD   PRINTED IN U.S.A.